Personal Injury Claims in Georgia:
The Definitive Guide for Injured Victims & Their Lawyers in Car Accident Cases

By:
Gary Martin Hays

ISBN: 978-0-9885523-5-7

For more information, please write:
We Published That, L.L.C.
c/o Adam Weart
PO Box 956669
Duluth, GA 30095

Dedication

As you enter the building for my law firm, you will see a plaque hanging on the exterior wall to the right of the front door. It is a quote from the book of Proverbs in the Old Testament:

> *"Speak up for those who cannot speak up for themselves, for the rights of all who are destitute. Speak up and judge fairly; defend the rights of the poor and needy."*

When I walk into the building, it is a reminder to me and my staff of the tremendous opportunity we have to help people - often times through the most difficult times they have ever faced. I dedicate this book to all of those clients - 32,000 and growing, who placed their confidence and trust in me and my staff to help them with their cases.

This book is also dedicated to the attorneys and staff at the Law Offices of Gary Martin Hays & Associates, P.C. - not only for all of the hard work that they perform for our clients, but for the manner in which they do that work. They exemplify their care and compassion every time they pick up the phone or meet with a client at the firm. None of this would be possible without their assistance, and for that, I am eternally grateful.

I also want to dedicate this book to my wife, Sheri, and our daughters, Audrey, Ashleigh and Ava. God Bless ALL of you for the love and support you have given me!

Gary Martin Hays

Table Of Contents

CHAPTER 1 - Introduction

In my 24 years of practicing law in the personal injury field, I have been involved in claims that would break your heart into pieces. When you investigate these wrecks and look at the photos taken at the scene of the crash - photos of men, women and children - who have died in these collisions, it leaves an indelible mark on you. Try as I may, I can never forget those faces.

Equally gut wrenching are the times when I meet with the surviving family members to talk about the wreck and about their loved one. They have such fond, vivid memories. But now, their world is turned upside down. I serve as part attorney and part counselor - helping them through the legal process while listening with them, at times crying with them, but always supporting them through the process.

Other families have met with me at the table discussing their wreck and their injuries. They tell me the paychecks have stopped coming because of the husband's back injury. Unfortunately, the bills haven't stopped. They are worried:

- will he lose his job?
- how will he pay the medical bills without health insurance?
- who will pay to repair the damaged car?
- what about his future medical needs?

These are certainly legitimate concerns and worries and these victims deserve answers. They deserve someone who is willing to fight to get them all the cash and benefits they are legally entitled to receive. Every single client needs an attorney that cares, that will take action, and will listen.

I'll admit - it's not an easy task. I suppose I learned best how to work with people when tragedy strikes from watching my father. For more than 50 years, he was a United Methodist Minister serving churches in south Alabama and northwest Florida. He was always there whenever someone needed to talk - never judging, but listening. It's funny how a lot of people just assume preachers only work on Saturdays for weddings and Sundays to preach - mix in the occasional funeral too. His work never seemed to end. If the home phone wasn't ringing, there was a knock on the door from one of the members of the church - or a friend of a friend who was a member - that just wanted to talk.

This kind of work is not a 9 to 5 type commitment. It requires long hours, rolling up the sleeves, and a dedicated work ethic. I am proud to say that we have helped over 29,000 victims and their families since 1993 in their car wreck, workers' compensation, wrongful death, inadequate security, and social security claims. It has been an honor and a privilege to have helped theses people through their trying times. I'm proud of what I do, and I'm thankful that the Good Lord has given me the opportunity to continue to work in this field.

It is my hope that this book will help guide injured victims and their attorneys through the mine fields that can exist in personal injury claims. Some attorneys would never let you peek behind the curtain to see how they handle cases. To me, there are no secrets. I want to share our knowledge with others so they can help Georgia's consumers take on the insurance industry and their "Delay, Deny and Defend" tactics.

Should you ever have any questions regarding the information contained in this book, please do not hesitate to contact me at Gary@GaryMartinHays.com. If you would like to have my law firm conduct a free, no obligation, completely confidential consultation of your case, please do not hesitate to call. At a minimum, if you don't call us, please call someone - but please call someone who specializes in personal injury claims.

Our toll free phone number is **1 (888) 934-8100**.

Or you can call **(770) 934-8000**.

One other note:

> The information we are sharing with you in this book is general in nature. It is not designed to provide specific legal advice regarding you and your potential claim. The information in this book may or may not apply to your specific case. Nothing can replace a consultation with an experienced attorney to discuss the facts about your particular claim. Further, should you have any desire to explore pursuing your potential claim, you should not delay as there are various statutes of limitation which could limit or completely bar your claims for recovery should you not pursue the matter in a timely fashion. We are NOT providing you information regarding the specific statute(s) of limitation applicable to your potential claim as this can only be determined after a detailed consultation of your case with an experienced attorney. By providing you with this information, we are not giving you specific legal advice about your case, nor have we been retained to handle your claim unless you and our firm have entered into a written contract of representation regarding your potential legal claim

I sincerely wish you all the best!

God Bless and Be Safe!

Gary Martin Hays
The Law Offices of
Gary Martin Hays & Associates, P.C.
3098 Breckinridge Boulevard
Duluth, GA 30096

CHAPTER 2 – Facts You Should Know About Car Wrecks

I've been practicing law since 1989 - strictly focusing my work on handling personal injury claims. People often ask me: "Isn't one car wreck case just like the next?" Their assumption is that if you handle one "rear-end collision case", then you will know how to handle all rear-end collision claims. This is simply not the case. EVERY case is different - from the parties involved, to the insurance adjusters, the defense lawyers, and even the judge. Experience in these types of cases helps you to navigate the sometimes treacherous waters to get fair compensation for your client.

But there are some things that haven't changed over the years. We can all quickly forget just how dangerous cars and trucks can be. When we get behind the wheel, we must remember we are driving a deadly weapon - one that can cause incredible havoc, death and destruction if we take our eyes off the road for a second to text on our phone or put in a new cd.

In this chapter, I want to give you some very important facts you should know about car wrecks. Hopefully, the information I share with you will cause you to pause a moment when you get in your car. You will be reminded to buckle up - and ask your passengers to do the same. You will not try to dial your phone or send a text message. Instead, you will operate your vehicle in as safe a manner as possible so you - and others - can safely make it to your destination.

Wrecks in Georgia:

According to the Governor's Office of Highway Safety, 2011 Annual Report, on Georgia's highways in 2010, there were:

- 1,244   fatalities
- 111,290   injuries
- 427   unrestrained fatalities
- 298   alcohol related fatalities
- 217   speed related fatalities
- 127   motorcycle fatalities
- 175   fatalities involving driver under age 21
- 168   pedestrian fatalities

According to the CDC, in the United States, there are over 30,000 people killed each year in crashes.[1] Further, in addition to the tragic loss of a loved one, these wrecks put another burden on the surviving family members. In 2005, crash deaths resulted in total losses in medical bills and lost wages of $41 billion dollars.[2] The CDC report also tells us that the specific costs of crash deaths in Georgia in 2005 was $1.55 billion dollars.[3]

Wrecks in the United States:

Here are some statistics from the National Highway Traffic Safety Administration's (NHTSA) 2009 Traffic Safety Annual Assessment:

- *33,808 total people killed*
- 13,095 killed in passenger car accidents
- 10,287 killed in light truck crashes
- 4,462 motorcycle deaths
- 4,092 pedestrians killed
- 630 Pedalcyclist deaths (in non-motorized vehicles, such as bicycles).

There are some other disturbing figures from this report. In addition to these fatalities, there were another 2.2 million people injured in highway crashes:

- 1.2 million drivers or occupants of passenger cars
- 759,000 drivers or passengers in light trucks
- 17,000 occupants of large trucks
- 90,000 motorcyclists
- 59,000 pedestrians
- 51,000 pedalcyclists

Older Adult Drivers:

There were 33 million licensed drivers in the US ages 65 and older in 2009.[4] It is certainly important that older adults have the ability to drive, get out of their home, and be independent. However, we need to understand that they are at a greater risk of being injured or killed in a wreck as they age.[5]

- In 2008, over 5,500 older adult drivers were killed in wrecks and more than 183,000 were injured in car crashes.[6]
-

To help reduce their risks while on the road, the CDC recommends that older adults take several steps:

- exercise regularly to increase strength, flexibility and reaction time
- have regular physical examinations, including eye examinations. If eyeglasses or contacts are prescribed, wear them.
- monitor your prescription medicine intake. Do not drive if the medication makes you drowsy or impairs your vision or reaction time.
- drive during daylight hours in good weather conditions.
- find the safest route, and one you will have no difficulty remembering.
- avoid distractions while driving.
- consider having a friend or relative drive you, or take other modes of transportation.

<u>Teen Drivers</u>:

According to the CDC, motor vehicle crashes are the leading cause of death for teenagers in the U.S.[7] "In 2010, about 2,700 teens in the United States aged 16-19 were killed and almost 282,000 were treated and released from emergency departments for injuries suffered in motor- vehicle crashes."[8] The ones most at risk are males. In 2010, the death rate from motor vehicle crashes for male drivers and their passengers was almost twice that of females.[9] The risk of a crash increases with the number of teen passengers in the vehicle.[10]

What can parents do to help insure the safety of their teen drivers?

The CDC tells us that "[R]esearch suggests that the most comprehensive graduated drivers licensing (GDL) programs are associated with reductions of 38% and 40% in fatal and injury crashes, respectively, among 16 year-old drivers."[11] This essentially means that the teens are not given a license and immediately released to drive whenever, wherever. They allow the teens to gradually adjust to driving conditions in low risk experiences, and then progress over time to lessen these restrictions.

Parents should also encourage their teen drivers to use seat belts! According to the CDC, "Compared with other age groups, teens have the lowest rate of seat belt use. In 2011, only 54% of high school students reported they always wear a seat belt when riding with someone else."[12] Make it a habit for yourself and your kids - any time you get in your car, buckle up. No exceptions!

Encourage your teen drivers not to drink and drive. First of all, if they are under 21, it is illegal for them to be drinking alcoholic beverages anyway. But if they are drinking, the last thing they need to do is get behind the wheel. The CDC tells us that "[I]n 2010, 22% of drivers aged 15 to 20 involved in fatal motor vehicle crashes were drinking."[13]

Speed kills. Encourage your teen driver to obey the speed limits on highways. This is especially important in neighborhood settings!

Child Passenger Safety:

According to the CDC, "[M]otor vehicle injuries are the leading cause of death among children in the United States."[14] In 2009 in the United States, 1,314 children ages 14 and younger died while being passengers in motor vehicle crashes; 179,000 were injured.[15] These are staggering statistics.

How can we protect our kids while riding in our vehicles?

- Use child safety seats! These can reduce the risk of death by 71% for infants, and by 54% for children between the ages of 1 - 4.[16]
- Use booster seats. When your child is too big for a child safety seat, use a booster. A report from the Children's Hospital of Philadelphia showed that booster seats reduce injury risks by 59% compared to just a seat belt for kids ages 4 - 7.[17]
- Never put a child in a seat with an airbag.
- Make sure that your child is properly buckled and in a child safety seat or booster seat that is appropriate for their age and size.

How can we be safer when we are behind the wheel?

At the end of this book is a free Bonus Chapter written by Gary Martin Hays & Derek Hays. This appeared in the best selling book they co-authored entitled "Consumer's Advocate: Today's Leading Attorneys Share Their Secrets on Finding Justice For Those Who've Been Wronged & Protecting Those In The Right." The chapter was entitled "The Mourning After: Helping Families Cope After A Drunk Driving Wreck."

In this chapter, we talk about our experience handling claims for injured victims, as well as for those who lost a loved one due to the negligence of a drunk driver. We also give you 3 ways you can protect yourself and family from being involved in a drunk driving collision. Additional advice is given to our readers on what to do if they have had too much to drink. I encourage you to take time to read this chapter as the information contained in it could help save a life - perhaps yours, or a member of your family.

Here are some basic rules in a nutshell:

- Don't drink and drive!
- Don't text and drive!
- If the phone call is that important to make or take, safely pull off the road.
- Don't engage in any activity when you are behind the wheel that would cause you to take your eyes off the road ahead - no matter how quick you think you can do it!
- Don't operate your vehicle if you are too sleepy to drive!
- Always wear your seat belt. Set a good example and habit for your children and make them buckle up as well.
- If they are still young enough and/or small enough to be in a child safety seat or booster seat, then put them in it.
- Obey all traffic laws. No speeding (especially in neighborhoods).

References

[1] CDC Feature: Cost of Deaths from Crashes (http://www.cdc.gov/features/CrashCosts/)
[2] Id.
[3] Id.
[4] Federal Highway Administration, Department of Transportation (US). Highway statistics 2009. Washington (DC): FHWA [cited 2011 Feb 25]

[5] National Highway Traffic Safety Administration, Department of Transportation (US). Traffic Safety Facts 2008: Older Population. Washington (DC): NHTSA; 2009 [cited 2011 Feb. 25].

[6] Id.

[7] Centers for Disease Control and Prevention, Web-based Injury Statistics Query and Reporting System (WISQARS) (2012).

[8] Id.

[9] Id.

[10] Chen L, Baker SP, Braver ER, Li G. Carrying passengers as a risk factor for crashes fatal to 16 - and 17 - year old drivers. JAMA 2000; 283 (12): 1578-82.

[11] Baker SP, Chen L, Li G. Nationwide review of graduated driver licensing. Washington (DC): AAA Foundation for Traffic Safety; 2007.

[12] Centers for Disease Control and Prevention. Youth Risk Behavior Surveillance System 2011 YRBS Data User's Guide [Online]. (2012).

[13] National Highway Transportation Safety Administration (NHTSA), Dept. Of Transportation (US). Traffic safety facts 2010: Young Drivers.

[14] CDC. Web-based Injury Statistics Query and Reporting System (http://www.cdc.gov/injury/wisqars [online]. National Center for Injury Prevention and Control, Centers for Disease Control and Prevention (producer) [2010 August 2].

[15] Department of Transportation (US), National Highway Traffic Safety Administration (NHTSA), Traffic Safety Facts 2008: Children. Washington (DC): NHTSA; 2009.

[16] Id.

[17] Committee on Injury, Violence, and Poison Prevention. Child passenger safety. Pediatrics. 2011; 127 (4): 788-93.

CHAPTER 3 - The Scene Of The Crash

No one ever wants to be involved in a wreck. It is not easy to think about - to prepare for something you never want to happen to you or to your family. But please ask yourself - will you know what to do if you are ever faced with this crisis?

This chapter will provide you with information you will need to know in the event you are involved in a collision. At the end of the chapter, there is a link to our website where you can print a checklist for you to place in the glove compartment of all of your vehicles. It will be a handy reference for you or any one of your family members to use if you are in a wreck.

Here are the **Top 8** things you need to do if you find yourself involved in a motor vehicle collision:

(1) **STOP YOUR VEHICLE**:

As soon as it is safe for you to do so, stop your vehicle. If it can be safely moved to the side of the road or a side street so you are not blocking the intersection, then move it over and turn off the ignition. Most states require you to do this, especially if the damage is minor, the car is driveable, and there are no injuries. Put on your hazard lights.

DO NOT LEAVE THE SCENE OF THE WRECK. If you leave the scene of the wreck - even if there are no injuries - you potentially expose yourself to some harsh consequences - both civil and criminal.

(2) **GET EMERGENCY MEDICAL HELP**!

Check all of the passengers in your vehicle to see if anyone is hurt. If you are able and it is safe for you to get out of your car, check on the driver and any passengers of the other vehicle(s) involved as well. If anyone is injured, call 911 immediately. If you have any kind of emergency notification device on your vehicle such as OnStar, activate it. Seconds can literally mean the difference between life and death with certain kinds of injuries. Stay calm.

DO NOT try and move anyone with visible injuries unless it is necessary to prevent further injury. If anyone is bleeding, attend to the wounds as best you can. It is a great idea to keep a first aid kit somewhere in your car. Apply pressure to any open wounds to try and stop the bleeding.

(3) **NOTIFY THE POLICE**

Call the police to come to the scene of the wreck to write up a report. It does not matter if you think it is a minor "fender bender". You need to have the wreck documented by the police in an accident report. It is a huge mistake to just exchange information with the other driver and leave. It may take a while for the police to arrive. Do not leave. It is extremely important for you to wait so you can insure you get as much information as possible about the driver of the other vehicle and their insurance, as well as a memorialization of what happened in the wreck.

(4) **DOCUMENT EVERYTHING**!

Get as much information from the other driver as possible (including all other drivers if additional vehicles are involved), such as:

- A full physical description of the other driver, including age, height, weight, clothing.
- Full name
- Home Address
- Home Phone Number
- Cell Phone Number
- Make, model, color, and year of other vehicle
- License plate
- Insurance information, including name of the insurance company, policy number, effective date of the policy, insured driver(s) and insured vehicle.

- If the driver of the other vehicle is not the owner, get the complete contact information for the owner.
- Get the names and contact information of any witnesses to the wreck. (It is also a good idea to write down their license plate information too).
- Make a note of the location of the wreck - including street names and any nearby intersections. It helps to sketch a scene of the wreck. This can include location of the vehicles before impact, and where they came to rest after the collision.
- Write down the full name and badge number of the investigating police officer. Often times, they will have a card to give you with this information printed on it.
- Write down the approximate time of the wreck.
- If you have a camera in your car, or if your cell phone has a camera, take pictures of the scene of the wreck, the vehicles involved (including a shot of the license plates), the damage to the vehicles, any debris from the vehicles, skid marks or gouge marks in the pavement, and any injuries. Make sure you protect these photos so they are not deleted from your camera. If you can do it without causing any additional problems, photograph the other driver and witnesses to the wreck. This can be done by "including" them in the background of some of the photos you take at the scene. It is a good idea to go ahead and have a copy made to your computer, or the images printed, so you do not lose this important information.
- If you are injured, DO NOT risk injuring yourself further by getting on the ground to take any photos. Imagine how that could be used against you by the defendant's insurance company.
- Does the driver of the other vehicle appear to be intoxicated or impaired in any way? If so, describe the behavior to the police officer and insist on further testing. Write down how you think the driver is impaired.
- If your vehicle has to be towed, get the information regarding the towing company, the tow truck driver, and the location your vehicle is being towed.

(5) **WATCH WHAT YOU SAY**!

When you speak with the driver of the other vehicle(s), you should first ask if they are injured. If so, contact 911 immediately. If not, you should only speak with them to get the information noted above. Nothing more. Do not admit responsibility for the wreck or say "I'm sorry" as this could potentially be used against you by their insurance company. Even if you think your actions contributed to cause the wreck, do not say anything. Negligence is a complicated legal issue. Even though you may think you were at fault to some degree, the law may not assess any legal blame to you for causing the wreck.

Do not make any kind of "agreement" with the driver at the scene. They may tell you that there is no need to call the police because the damages are minor. Or they may tell you they will cover all damages instead of letting their insurance company deal with it. Nothing good ever comes out of those "agreements". Your physical injuries or the damage to your car could be far greater than you may realize. Also, if you delay notifying the other insurance company because of this side agreement gone bad, the coverage for that wreck may be lost because the insurer did not receive timely notice of the accident.

Do not blame the other driver - even if it is very clear that they were at fault - as this could start an argument at the scene of the wreck. If the other driver admits they were responsible for causing the wreck, make a note of what they said. Also try to memorialize anything else they tell you, such as "I was on my way from work", or "I was leaving my job trying to hurry to pick up my dry cleaning before the store closed." All of their statements could be very important.

It is important that you fully cooperate with the police at the scene of the wreck, but again - DO NOT ACCEPT FAULT for the wreck. You will be under a lot of stress at the scene of the wreck. You may not be thinking clearly and assume facts that are not true. Statements you make can also be misunderstood or misinterpreted. If it is the right thing to do later, you can always accept responsibility after you calm down, leave the scene, and discuss the details of the wreck with your attorney.

Do not argue with the police officer at the scene! Nothing good can ever come from that conduct.

Also remember that it is NEVER a good idea to get involved in any kind of verbal altercation with the driver - and especially no physical altercation. Your conduct at the scene of the claim can positively or negatively affect the outcome of our claim. Be professional and courteous to everyone!

(6) **NOTIFY YOUR INSURANCE AGENT AND INSURANCE COMPANY**

It is important that you notify your insurance agent and the company insuring the vehicle that was involved in the wreck as soon as possible - even if you do not plan on filing any kind of claim with them. You may think the other person's insurance is valid only to find out later the policy had been canceled. If you delay in notifying your company, you could be jeopardizing coverage. Document the names and phone numbers of everyone that you speak with at your agent's office, as well as the insurance company, should you need this information in the future.

Your insurance company may require a recorded statement. Most insurance contracts require that you cooperate fully with their investigation of the claim, including providing a recorded interview. One suggestion though - if you are injured, I highly recommend having your attorney present with you or on the phone with you during this recorded statement.

(7) **Notify the At Fault Party's Insurance Company**

It is always best to have your attorney notify the other party's insurance company about the wreck. If you do not have an attorney, you should do it. Give them the basics about what happened in the wreck. Do not consent to a recorded statement until you speak with a lawyer about your case. If you were hurt in the wreck, you can disclose this to the insurance company. However, I highly recommend you also tell them you do not know the full extent of your injuries and medical bills. When you have completed your treatment, supporting materials documenting all of your claims will be provided to them. It is also important to let them know the location of your vehicle so they can send a property damage appraiser to look at it to assess the repair costs.

DO NOT SIGN anything unless and until you have an attorney review it. This includes any property damage releases, or any piece of paper that allows the insurance company full access to your medical records. Your lawyer can provide them all relevant medical records when you have completed your treatment.

(8) **Get your stuff!**

If you have valuables in your vehicle, and you can take them out and with you, then do it. Sadly, these items will often come up "missing" when the vehicle is towed to a storage lot. It is safer not to take a chance and have the items removed. If you are physically unable, maybe a family member or friend can quickly help you retrieve these items from your vehicle.

BEWARE:

- Some insurance companies are now dispatching their claims adjusters to the scene of the wreck. These adjusters will try to take your statement at the scene. They may even have authority to make you a minimal offer on the spot of $500.00 to settle all of your injury claims. I highly recommend you consider rejecting this offer. If you are hurt, there is no way you can know the full severity of your injuries moments after the collision. We have received too many calls from people who have settled their claims for this low amount, only to find out they had injuries that would require medical testing and treatment costing thousands of dollars. They were stuck with these bills because they settled ALL claims. Do not fall for this trap!

- Do not hire ANY attorney that contacts you after your wreck. This is unethical. These attorneys may have someone reach out to you on behalf of their office to try and get you to retain their services. These people are known as "runners." The attorneys that engage in this type of practice should be turned over to the State Bar of Georgia. You will not be helping your case - and in fact, you could seriously be jeopardizing any successful recovery in your claim if you hire a lawyer or law firm that uses runners.

- The same can be written about chiropractors or medical clinics that contact you after a wreck. If you have health insurance coverage, we suggest you consider using that coverage to seek out a health care provider to treat you for your injuries. Keep in mind - the at fault party's insurance company usually will not pay for your medical treatment as you incur your medical bills. If you do not have health insurance, this is yet another reason why you should consult with an attorney.

****

Author's note: Twenty minutes after I completed this chapter, I left my office to drive to my home. A driver cut across three lanes of traffic and hit the front passenger side of my vehicle. He pulled over into a gas station parking lot and I followed him. I immediately called 911 and told them there were no injuries, but we did want an officer to come to the scene to write a report.

We waited for approximately 45 minutes for an officer to arrive. This was not an extraordinary long time as the wreck occurred at the peak of rush hour. The other driver did ask me if he could just leave me all of his information before the police arrived as he was late for an appointment. I told him I appreciated the predicament he was in, but he had to stay. I could see how a younger driver or someone less inclined to stand up to this man could have been brow beaten into allowing him to leave.

When the police did arrive, he tried to place the blame on me since "I hit him." The officer took statements from both of us, surveyed the scene, and quickly told the driver he was at fault for failing to yield from a private drive. If I had allowed him to leave, he more than likely would have contested everything. This could have delayed me getting my car repaired.

So lesson learned - make sure everyone stays at the scene of the wreck so a full report can be taken from all drivers, passengers, and other witnesses when possible.

****

Here is the link to the car wreck checklist:

http://www.garymartinhays.com/img/CarAccidentChecklist.pdf

CHAPTER 4 – Investigating The Wreck

It is extremely important that a complete and thorough investigation of the wreck occur as quickly as possible. Evidence can be lost. The skid marks at the scene of the wreck could be washed away by rain. Witnesses may not remember as many details if they are not contacted soon after the wreck.

With our firm, the investigation of the potential claim starts from the first moment the potential client calls our office or comes in for their free consultation. We interview the client to find out as many details as possible about the wreck. We also review the police report and verify its accuracy based upon our client's statement of what happened.

If we agree to represent the client, a contract of employment is signed authorizing our firm to act as the legal representative for the client in all matters related to the car wreck. We then take further actions, as necessary, to investigate the claim, including:

- interviewing the investigating the police officers that responded to the wreck;
- interviewing potential witnesses;
- hiring an accident reconstructionist to go to the scene of the wreck, take measurements and photos, so he can render an opinion on how the collision happened, including the speed of the vehicles;
- obtaining other incident reports if additional government agencies investigated the collision;
- checking with businesses in the area to see if any of the collision was caught on their surveillance cameras;
- contacting local police agencies to see if they had any "red light" cameras at the intersection that could have captured the collision on film;

- checking with businesses or homes near the scene of the collision to see if anyone saw the wreck or came to the scene to render aid after it occurred;
- interviewing EMT's and any other first responders that treated the persons involved in the wreck;
- interviewing the tow truck driver(s) that removed the vehicles from the scene;
- speaking with the mechanics that repaired the vehicle;
- attending any hearings or trials that will happen if the Defendant was cited for crimes other than the traffic violation, such as for Driving Under the Influence;
- requesting a certified disposition of the Defendant's traffic citation.

As the case progresses, we may find out that additional experts may need to retained to investigate other facts. This is where experience really helps as an attorney who has not handled a lot of these claims can waste an inordinate amount of time and money investigating ancillary issues that do not matter instead of focusing on the ones that do. Also, it is wrong to assume that the investigation only occurs at the beginning of the case. We are constantly researching facts and that law that may add value to our client's claim - even if we are in the midst of a trial.

****

Note for Attorneys:

A sample questionnaire is attached for your review in the "Forms" section at the end of this book. This is the most basic checklist that we use when we start our initial evaluation of a claim. Once you have completed this with your client, please do not forget about it and just put it in the file. I highly recommend you use this questionnaire to help formulate a "to do" list. Prioritize other things that need to be done to make sure you can place liability squarely on the defendant, and that you locate all other sources of insurance available to your client.

CHAPTER 5 – Property Damage: Total Losses, Repairs, and Diminished Value

This chapter will help address a lot of questions and concerns that you will have regarding the property damage aspect of your claim. It is bad enough that you have suffered personal injuries caused by an accident. Damage to your vehicle can also become a pain if you do not know what to do or how to do it. If your car was damaged in a wreck, it is our hope this information will be helpful in educating you about your rights and obligations when seeking repair of your car.

We have broken down the chapter into the following sections:

(1)   Towing & Storage

(2)   Repairs

(3)   Rental Car

(4)   Total Loss

(5)   Salvage

(6)   Uh Oh - I'm Upside Down

(7)   Diminished Value

PLEASE NOTE:

The information we are sharing with you in this book is general in nature, and not designed to provide specific legal advice regarding you and your potential claim. The summary listed below may or may not apply to your specific case. Nothing can replace a consultation with an experienced attorney to discuss the facts about your particular claim. Further, should you have any desire to explore pursuing your potential claim, you should not delay as there are various statutes of limitation which could limit or completely bar your claims for recovery should you not pursue the matter in a timely fashion. We are NOT providing you information regarding the specific statute(s) of limitation applicable to your potential claim as this can only be determined after a detailed consultation of your case with an experienced attorney. By providing you with this information, we are not giving you specific legal advice about your case, nor have we been retained to handle your claim unless you and our firm have entered into a written contract of representation regarding your potential legal claim. Should you have any questions regarding a potential claim, please contact us right away at (770) 934-8000 or toll free, 1-888-934-8100.

Before we address the different topics in this chapter, it is VITALLY IMPORTANT to mention something else. We suggest that you deal with the Insurance Claims Adjuster in a professional and courteous manner for a lot of reasons, even if they may act like the most condescending horse's rear end you have ever encountered. Your goal is to get your vehicle repaired in an effective and timely manner. If the vehicle is a total loss, your goal is to get the most money you possibly can for your property damage loss. It is our hope this goal can be accomplished without litigation, which is costly, and very time consuming. A certain level of cooperation and understanding may prove to be crucial in obtaining the best possible settlement for you.

Let me give you an example:

> Imagine if you are trying to get the best possible settlement on your car if it is a total loss in a wreck. I would respectfully suggest that it might not be a good idea to walk into the insurance company's office, kick the adjuster in the shin, tell him he does not know what he is doing, and then say "give

me the most money you can on this car, buddy." I believe that dealing with the adjuster in as courteous a manner as is reasonably possible will significantly contribute to the possibility of resolving your property damage claims as quickly and effectively as possible.

1.   <u>TOWING & STORAGE</u>:

Who is going to pay if your car needs to be towed from the scene of a wreck?

If you were hurt and taken away by ambulance, your car was probably towed to the nearest wrecker yard. Your car may be inoperable because of the severity of damage. Either way, you will be faced with towing and storage costs. The answer to the question of "Who pays?" depends on you being able to prove the other driver is at fault for the wreck. This is often referred to by the legal phrase "Who is liable?" If the other side was at fault - if they breached a legal duty to you - that party may be held liable.

We shall assume that the other driver caused the wreck and is liable for your injuries and property damage. There may be times when the other driver is given the ticket for causing the wreck, but the insurance company will want to fight it based on other witness testimony or legal loopholes. It is our hope this is not the case in your claim.

If your car is towed from the scene of the wreck, YOU are ultimately responsible for the bill if the liability insurer does not accept responsibility for the wreck. Plain and simple. The towing company and the storage lot will look to you for payment. When you go to the storage lot to get your vehicle, they will ask you to pay the charges in full before they will release it. Therefore, it is important to get in touch with the property damage adjuster for the other at fault driver as quickly as possible so they can arrange payment of your towing and storage charges so you will not have to pay.

Under **O.C.G.A. Section 33-7-11.1**, every insurance company licensed to issue an automobile policy in Georgia must have coverage for the benefit of a third party claimant for loss of use and towing and storage costs. The insurer's duty to pay under this statute is triggered when they accept liability on behalf of their insured - the at fault driver.

Once your car is towed to a storage facility, the daily charges will add up very quickly. You should look to the other driver's insurance company to also pay for all storage charges from the day of the wreck to the time the insurance company authorizes release of your car for repairs.

> WARNING: If you delay in any way the repair of your car because you are fighting with the insurance company over who is at fault or some other issue, YOU may be personally liable for any storage charges incurred. You have an obligation to *MITIGATE* (or lessen) your damages. You do not need to leave your car in storage for five weeks at the storage yard and expect the insurance company to pay for these charges.

How can you *MITIGATE* your damages? If you have collision coverage, you should immediately contact YOUR insurance company to pay for towing, storage, and rental car expenses if the at-fault party's insurance company is balking at paying. You DO NOT want to wait for a determination of liability while the storage fees mount.

What is *collision coverage?* Collision coverage is optional and available to cover damages done to the insured vehicle. This is usually limited to damage as a result of an impact with another vehicle or object. Collision coverage will allow you to get your damaged vehicle repaired - even if you caused the wreck. But please note - collision coverage is not required in Georgia. Also, collision coverage does not usually cover events where the vehicle is damaged because of fire, theft, striking an animal, vandalism, falling objects, or because of the weather - like hail or flood damage. These losses are usually covered under comprehensive coverage.

What should you do to get your collision coverage to apply? Call your insurance company and notify them of the wreck IMMEDIATELY. Complete an accident report for them -- which often times is taken over the phone. The insurer may also ask for a copy of the police incident report. Once this is done, your adjuster will give you instructions regarding the property damage claim.

If you still have personal items in your car, you have the right to remove them from your vehicle at the storage lot - provided you can supply proof that you own the car. The storage lot may even have someone go to the car with you. When you go to the lot to get any items, make sure you obtain an accurate receipt of every thing you remove from the vehicle.

TAKE PICTURES:

A picture is worth a thousand words (and sometimes thousands of dollars). Take pictures of the property damage to your car. If the other driver's vehicle is at the lot, take pictures of it as well - especially if there is extensive damage. Don't be cheap. Take pictures from different angles so you can pick out the best photos that show all the damage to your car.

2.   REPAIRS:

Now the insurance company has taken responsibility for their driver causing the wreck. What happens next? If your car can be repaired, it needs to be taken to the repair facility. And we are often asked this question - "Do I have to get my car repaired where the insurance company tells me it needs to be fixed?" The answer is NO. You can get it fixed at the body shop of your choice. In fact, Georgia law prohibits an insurer from restricting you to use one of their selected repair facilities. Further, they cannot threaten to withhold payment on your claim because you chose your own repair shop. (See **O.C.G.A. Section 33-34-6**.) We do suggest that you find a reputable shop experienced in handling cars like yours. You can call the dealership that sold you the vehicle for a recommendation. Your own insurance agent may know of a good repair facility as well.

When the car is at your selected repair facility, they will perform an appraisal of the damages to the car. The insurance adjuster and the repair facility will decide what needs to be fixed, and how much it will cost. Once the adjuster, you, and the repair shop agree on the charges, the work is then performed on your car.

When your car is repaired, the insurance company will often times cut a check directly to you and the body shop. It should be your goal (and the body shop's), to have your car in the same condition it was in BEFORE the wreck. It is important that you perform a COMPLETE examination and evaluation of your car before you sign anything! Also, make sure that if the check for the repairs is made payable to you and the body shop, that you endorse the check as follows:

"For property damage ONLY; not a full and final settlement as other damages may be discovered; not a settlement of diminished value."

This may cover you in the event another item needs to be repaired, or was repaired inadequately. However - it is difficult, sometimes impossible, and often too expensive to try to prove months later that a certain problem you are now having with your car was due to the wreck. You may want to consider hiring an appraiser at *your expense* to evaluate and document the condition of your following its repair.

3.   RENTAL CAR:

What do you do while your car is being repaired? You are entitled to a replacement vehicle. The at fault driver's insurance company will either pay for your rental, or reimburse you for your "loss of use" of your vehicle while it is being repaired. But please understand — the "replacement" or "rental" vehicle DOES NOT necessarily have to equal your car in value or quality. The reimbursement cost could run between $20.00 per day to $35.00 per day - depending on the insurer. You may upgrade to a nicer vehicle, but you may be responsible for the difference.

If the other person's insurance company is still contesting liability, you may have to file using your insurance if you have "Rental" coverage on your policy. Again, you must *mitigate* your damages if liability is contested. If you have this coverage through your insurer, you must notify them immediately and ask them to supply you with a rental car.

When you get the rental vehicle, you are required to show proof of insurance when you sign the rental agreement. Many companies will not rent to people under the age of 25. They will often require you to leave a credit card number just in case the insurance company revokes the rental, or you incur excess charges beyond what the insurance company will pay.

> WARNING: If your car is found to be a total loss, the insurance company will often times not extend your rental loss beyond the date they make you an offer to settle your property damage claim.

> For example: Your car is found to be a total loss. The insurance company offers you $4,500.00 as settlement for your lost vehicle. You think the value is $5,000.00, and you want to hold out for the extra $500.00. The insurance company will typically stop paying for rental once the offer is made. At most, they will extend the rental for a day or two. You may be responsible for any additional days you have the rental vehicle.

4.   <u>TOTAL LOSS</u>:

There really is not a set rule that all insurance companies use in determining when a car is a "total loss." Some companies use a "70%" figure. For example, if the cost of repairing your damaged vehicle is 70% or greater of the fair market value of your vehicle, then they will usually determine it is a total loss. When that happens, the insurance company will issue a check to you and any lien holder(s) for the fair market value of the vehicle before the wreck. You then sign the car over to the insurance company and they will in turn sell it to a salvage yard.

How can you determine what the fair market value of your vehicle was before the wreck? There are couple of sites on the internet that will allow you to do some research:

www.nadaguides.com

www.edmunds.com

Another method is getting a copy of the Sunday newspaper, as well as copy of any free auto trader magazine you can pick up at the grocery store. Look for comparable vehicles to yours. You can use this as evidence to support your claims with the adjuster that the car is worth more than what they are offering.

What about any additional upgrades that you added to the car? Document, document, document. It is extremely important that you provide proof of any add-on items that may increase the value of the vehicle. This could include receipts, purchase orders, or work orders. The fact that you just had the oil changed or the air conditioner repaired does not increase the fair market value of the car as you would expect the car to be in proper working order before the wreck. But if you put in a new, upgraded stereo system and speakers, the insurance company will consider this if you are able to provide proof of purchase and reasonable proof of value.

5. SALVAGE:

What happens if you want to keep the car and have the insurance company pay you for the total loss? You will need to find out how much a salvage yard would give you for your car, and then negotiate with the insurance company on a fair amount for the totaled vehicle.

For example:

> You have a car with a fair market value of $8,000.00. The salvage value is only $2,000.00 after the wreck. The insurance company should give you $6,000.00 for the total loss of the car. This is the fair market value ($8,000.00) minus the salvage value ($2,000.00).

But after you have settled and kept the salvaged car, you will be responsible for towing your car to another location, paying any storage costs, and repairing or disposing of the car. Plus, if you plan on repairing your car, you will have to get the title changed to reflect that the car was a total loss. This is required so anyone that may purchase the vehicle at a later date will be on notice of the prior wreck and repairs. In our opinion, unless you have extensive experience in this area, the less hassle approach is to accept the check for the total loss of your car and let the insurance company deal with the vehicle and salvage.

6. UH OH - I'M UPSIDE DOWN

If you owe more to a creditor for the car than what the car is worth (the fair market value), you are "upside down" in your vehicle. In these days of "ZERO PERCENT FINANCING" and 60 month loans, we see a lot of people in this situation. The longer the term of the car note, the more affordable the monthly payments. But the end result may be that you pay $25,000.00 over time for a vehicle that is only worth $12,500.00 at the time you bought it.

But here is the problem:

> If your car is totaled, and the fair market value is only
> $5,000.00, yet you owe the creditor $10,000.00, the
> insurance company WILL NOT pay off your car note. They
> will just pay your creditor/lien holder the fair market value
> for your car - $5,000.00. You are still responsible for paying
> your creditor the extra $5,000.00. And you still owe the
> creditor this money even though you do not have the car any
> more.

What can you do?

- Avoid this situation on the front end. Don't try to buy more
  car than you can realistically afford. BEWARE the financing
  traps that place you in this predicament!
- See if you can purchase "Gap" insurance when you buy the
  vehicle. Essentially, gap insurance will pay off the excess
  balance on the car note in the event of a total loss.
- See if the creditor will work with you on rolling this balance
  into the purchase of another vehicle. But this solution may
  only cause you the same problem down the road if you are in
  another wreck. Think long and hard before you decide on
  this option.

There is no way to politely put this. The insurance company DOES
NOT CARE how much
you owe to your creditor for your vehicle. Their only concern is
"What is the fair market
value of the vehicle?"

7.   DIMINISHED VALUE:

I want to expose one of the best kept secrets in the insurance
industry. The insurance companies

are saving literally hundreds of millions of dollars each year right here in Georgia because of this secret. This money should be paid to Georgia's consumers. But like most things, if the person doesn't know they are entitled to receive this money, the insurance company is not going to knock on their door and voluntarily hand it to them.

What is this secret? It's called a "diminished value claim." Let me explain what that means. If you are involved in a car wreck, your car will suffer property damage. When you get your car repaired, you know it will be worth less than it was before the wreck. Think of it this way. If you walk onto a used car lot and you saw two identical cars parked side by side. One had never been wrecked, and one had been wrecked and repaired. Most people would never buy the car that had been repaired. You don't want to buy someone else's problem. And if you would even consider buying the car that had been wrecked, you would want a substantial discount.

Diminished value is what the market says your vehicle lost in value because of the repairs.

How do you calculate the amount of diminished value? The best way to do it is by hiring an appraiser to do a market survey for your car. And this is where the insurance companies are misleading consumers. A lot of insurance companies use a ridiculous formula the industry created to calculate diminished value. They make it sound like it is a fair and reasonable method but it is not.

Let me give you an example of how the insurance companies are not being fair:

One insurance company sent my client a check for $496.00 using their formula. We hired an independent appraiser. His market survey showed the vehicle lost $2,235.00 in diminished value. The insurance company was trying to cheat my client out of over $1700. This isn't right.

And they get away with this every day here in Georgia. It's time we stop them.

Let's do some math here to further illustrate just how badly the insurance industry is screwing over Georgia consumers. There are on average approximately 350,000 car wrecks in Georgia each year. Now remember, the cars in some of those wrecks will be total losses so they will not be repaired and will not have a diminished value claim. But let's just say only 150,000 are repaired. If the insurance company is holding on to a minimum of $1,000 on each of those claims that they would ordinarily have to pay out, they are taking $150 million out of the pockets of Georgia's consumers.

It does not matter who is at fault in the wreck for you to be able to pursue a diminished value claim. If you are at fault in causing the wreck, you can still pursue a diminished value claim against your insurance company. If someone else causes the wreck, you can pursue the claim against their company. Either way, if your car is wrecked and repaired, you have a diminished value claim and should pursue it.

****

The following material is taken from a paper and presentation I delivered to a large audience of attorneys in Destin, Florida, in 2011, regarding diminished value claims at the Georgia Trial

Lawyers' Annual Auto Torts Seminar:

In 2009, I was driving around the Discover Mills Shopping Center when a car in front of me stopped. I stopped, but the young woman driving her dad's truck that was traveling behind me was not as attentive. She slammed into the back of my car. I was driving a 2006 Mercedes CLK 350 convertible. The wreck caused approximately $6,500.00 in property damage to the rear of the car.

Before the wreck, the car was in great condition. I kept up with the maintenance schedule suggested by the manufacturer - kept the oil changed, tires rotated, etc. It had never been damaged before this incident. I was thankful that no one was hurt, but was ticked that my car had lost value because of the wreck.

A good friend of mine, who also happened to be an attorney, suggested I pursue a diminished value claim. I thanked him for his kind words but told him I did not have the time to deal with it. He politely agreed to handle the claim for me. He had an appraisal performed on my car, sent a demand to the insurance company, and within 60 days, had a check for me in the amount of $3,950.00 - the full amount of the diminished value appraisal. I quickly realized I needed to learn more about these claims.

The information and material I am sharing with you is the compilation of 2 years of work - not just by me, but by many amazing attorneys who have been willing to freely share their work product, their thoughts, and their time on these claims

WHAT IS DIMINISHED VALUE?

It is the loss in market value of a car **after** it has been wrecked and repaired.

Here is another way to look at it: Assume two identical cars are side by side on a car lot. One has been wrecked and repaired, and the other has never been wrecked and repaired. Diminished value is what the market says it expects Joe Consumer would want in a discount before he would be willing to buy the wrecked and repaired car vs. the one that has never been wrecked.

Exhibit A

2008 Nissan Altima

Vehicle #1 - Never Wrecked   Vehicle #2 - Wrecked and Repaired

Which vehicle would you want to purchase?   According to a recent survey, 55% of consumers say they would NEVER buy a vehicle that has been wrecked and repaired. 81% said they would buy it ONLY if they were given a LARGE discount. Most consumers do not want to buy someone else's problem.

Example #1:

Our client owned a 2008 Nissan Altima that sustained rear end damage in a wreck in October, 2009. Her car had approximately 34,000 miles on it at the time of the wreck. The vehicle was in great condition. She kept up with the manufacturer's maintenance program, such as oil changes, tire rotations, etc. Her car had never been damaged in any way prior to the wreck.

As a result of the wreck, the property damage was a little over $10,000.00.

Exhibit B:

2008 Nissan Altima

Vehicle #1 - Never Wrecked

Vehicle #2 - Wrecked and Repaired
*FRAME DAMAGE
*Over 111.3 hours to repair
 -including 26 hours of refinishing/painting
 -8.4 hours mechanical
*Damage to 10 panels:
 -right quarter panel
 -left quarter panel
 -left corner panel
 -left wheelhouse
 -luggage lid
 -rear body panel
 -rear floor plan
 -right rear sidemember
 -left rear sidemember
 -rear bumper

Put those cars side by side on a car lot and see how this will appear to a consumer:

Which vehicle would you want to purchase?   According to this insurer's method of computing diminished value, the consumer would buy that wrecked and repaired car if you discounted it only $572.63.

Exhibit C:

Several insurance companies use some variation of a formula known as 17c to calculate diminished value. Exhibit C demonstrates the lunacy of this formula. They argue with a straight face that a consumer would buy a vehicle with a NADA value of $15,775.00 before the wreck that sustained over $10,000 in property damage, including FRAME DAMAGE, and required over 111 hours to repair, if the seller would reduce the price of the car by only $572.63.

In this claim, we hired an independent appraiser to assess the diminished value of our client's Nissan Altima. He did an appraisal of the vehicle BEFORE the wreck and then AFTER the wreck and repairs. He opined the Nissan Altima sustained an inherent diminished value loss of $3,550.00.

Exhibit D:

2008 Nissan Altima

Value Before the Wreck	Value After the Wreck and Repairs	Diminished Value of
$16,500	$12,950	$3,550.00

What is the proper method for calculating diminished value? Both the first party and third party statutes are silent on this issue, but there is guidance for us in the case law.

According to <u>Canal Ins. Co. v. Tullis</u>, 237 Ga. App. 515, 516-17(1999), where damage to a vehicle is not a total loss, a party seeking to recover for damage to the vehicle has two options in proving the amount of damage. These choices of proof are:

1. The difference between the fair market value of the vehicle before and after the collision; and
2. The reasonable costs of repair, together with hire on the vehicle while rendered incapable of use and the value of any additional permanent impairment, provided that the aggregate of such amounts does not exceed the fair market value before the collision.

See <u>Myers v. Thornton</u>, 224 Ga. App. 326, 480 S.E.2d 334 (1997).

"There are two ways to prove damages to a motor vehicle caused by a collision. One alternative is by showing the difference between the fair market value of the vehicle before the collision as compared with the market value of the damaged vehicle after the collision. Damages may also be proved by proof of the reasonable value of labor and material used for necessary repairs that are the direct and proximate result of the collision, together with hire on the vehicle while rendered incapable of use, plus the value of any permanent impairment in the value of the vehicle." Id. at 326. See also Archer v. Monroe, 165 Ga.App. 724, 302 S.E.2d 583 (1983); Sykes v. Sin, 229 Ga.App. 155, 493 S.E.2d 571 (1997).

FIRST PARTY DV CLAIMS

A.   Statute:

The statute that authorizes first party diminished value claims is **O.C.G.A. Section 33-4-6**:

(a) In the event of a loss which is covered by a policy of insurance and the refusal of the insurer to pay the same within 60 days after a demand has been made by the holder of the policy and a finding has been made that such refusal was in bad faith, the insurer shall be liable to pay such holder, in addition to the loss, not more than 50 percent of the liability of the insurer for the loss or $5,000.00, whichever is greater, and all reasonable attorney's fees for the prosecution of the action against the insurer. The action for bad faith shall not be abated by payment after the 60 day period nor shall the testimony or opinion of an expert witness be the sole basis for a summary judgment or directed verdict on the issue of bad faith. The amount of any reasonable attorney's fees shall be determined by the trial jury and shall be included in any judgment which is rendered in the action; provided, however, the attorney's fees shall be fixed on the basis of competent expert evidence as to the reasonable value of the services based on the time spent and legal and factual issues involved in accordance with prevailing fees in the locality where the action is pending; provided, further, the trial court shall have the discretion, if it finds the jury verdict fixing attorney's fees to be greatly excessive or inadequate, to review and amend the portion of the verdict fixing attorney's fees without the necessity of disapproving the entire verdict. The limitations contained in this Code section in reference to the amount of attorney's fees are not controlling as to the fees which may be agreed upon by the plaintiff and the plaintiff's attorney for the services of the attorney in the action against the insurer.

B.   Nuts and Bolts

How can you prove the diminished value of your client's vehicle? There is a code section under Georgia law that deals specifically with "value." According to **O.C.G.A. Section 24-9-66**:

> "Direct testimony as to market value is in the nature of *opinion* evidence. One need not be an expert or dealer in the article in question but may testify as to its value if he has had an opportunity for forming a correct opinion."

You can prove diminished value through an expert, through a dealer, or through someone else - including the owner - as long as you can show that person "had an opportunity for forming a correct opinion."

Here are my suggestions:

(1)   Hire an independent appraiser to evaluate the vehicle.

(2)   In addition to the independent appraisal, have your client take the final repair bill to CarMax. Your client should provide them with a copy of the complete repair bill and ask them to appraise the vehicle and get your client an offer on the vehicle. Have your client get the appraiser's card. When they come back with an appraisal and offer, tell your client to get

detailed and specific reasons from the appraiser as to the basis for their offer. Make sure your client takes notes.

But isn't this hearsay? Yes, but . . .

See Apostle v. Prince, 158 Ga.App. 56, 279 S.E.2d 304 (1981):

> "In order for a witness to give his opinion as to value, he must give his reasons for forming that opinion by showing that he has some knowledge, experience, or familiarity as to the value of the item." Citing Toney v. Johns, 153 Ga. App. 880, 881, 267 S.E.2d 298 (1980). Evidence of value is not to be excluded merely because the valuation fixed by the witness as a matter of opinion depends . . . wholly or in part upon hearsay, provided the witness has had an opportunity of forming a correct opinion. If it is based on hearsay this would merely go to its weight and not be a ground for valid objections."

See also B&L Service Co. v. Gerson, 167 Ga.App. 679, 307 S.E.2d 262 (1983):

> "Evidence of value is not to be excluded merely because the valuation fixed by the witness as a matter of opinion depends on hearsay, hence the testimony of the witness is not objectionable for the reason stated. Market value may rest wholly or in part upon hearsay, provided the witness has had an opportunity of forming a correct opinion. If it is based on hearsay this would go merely to its weight and would not be a ground for valid objections."

       ****

There are so many cases standing for the proposition that even though the testimony is based in whole or in part on hearsay, as long as the witness can show he/she had an opportunity to form a correct opinion, then it will be admissible.

I'd suggest making sure your client can - at a minimum - lay a factual basis for the opinion of the value of the car by knowing these factors:

- Date and purchase price of the car
- Options on the vehicle
- Condition of the car at the time of purchase
- Mileage of the vehicle at the time of wreck
- Maintenance history on the car
- Any new upgrades on the car since the date of purchase
- New tires immediately before wreck
- Any prior wrecks or damage repairs
- Value of car at the time of wreck based upon AJC Cars, NADA Guides, Edmunds, or by asking the dealer about the value of the car immediately BEFORE the wreck.
- Make sure they are educated on what repairs were made to their car and why.
- How many hours were spent repairing the car; number of panels damaged, repaired, and replaced?
- Frame damage?
- Amount of paint required?
- Were airbags deployed, repaired/replaced?
- Did the repair facility use OEM parts (Original Equipment from the Manufacturer) or other parts? There may be some warranty issues if non-OEM parts are used.
- Knowledge of the amount of the repair costs?
- Be able to offer testimony about the condition of the vehicle post-repairs.

For example, even though the repair facility did everything possible to restore the vehicle to its pre-loss condition, the vehicle still has problems:

- car noises are now present either from the engine or within the passenger compartment;
- the vehicle does not track down the road like it did pre-wreck;
- braking is not as smooth;
- obvious paint discrepancies in trying to get repaired panels to match original panels.
- Be able to testify re: efforts to get quotes re: value of vehicle post-wreck and repair from dealer and CarMax facility.

(3) Once you have the appraisal in place, prepare a demand to send to the insurance carrier.

Under the statute, you must give the carrier 60 days to review the demand **BEFORE** a lawsuit can be filed. You can not shorten the time period. If the insurer asks to inspect the vehicle, allow them to do it but stress it must be done within the 60 day time period. You do not want them to use your client's failure to cooperate as a defense to the bad faith claims.

Keep track of what the insurer does within that 60 day time period. Did they speak with your appraiser? Did they ask for additional information from you?

If an offer is made, write them a letter asking for the basis of their offer. If they hired an independent appraiser, demand a copy of it.

(4)   If the insurer does not make a reasonable offer at the expiration of the 60 day time period, then file suit. No exceptions. The more attorneys that are holding these insurers accountable, the better it will be for all of Georgia's consumers.

C.   <u>Tips</u>

- I highly suggest filing in State or Superior Court. This will allow you to send discovery to the insurance company and both the defendant driver and the defendant insurance company in 3rd party claims.
- Always send a letter to the adjuster asking how they calculated the diminished value. If it is based upon an appraiser's report, ask for a copy of the report. Let them know you need it within the 60 day TIME LIMIT DEMAND.
- If they ask to inspect the vehicle, allow them this opportunity. But again, in writing, stress to them the importance of doing it within the 60 day TIME LIMIT DEMAND.
- If they make any new offers, write them a letter asking them the basis for their new offer. Make them document it. If they don't, hound them about it in writing to establish their continuing bad faith.
- If offers are made outside the 60 day TIME LIMIT DEMAND, and you have filed suit, make sure you file a Motion In Limine to exclude these as offers of compromise.
- If a lawsuit is filed, look to see when the diminished value was calculated by the adjuster. One insurance company's "Auto Claims Manual" states that diminished value should not be assessed until all the repairs are completed. See what the total amount of the repairs were that the adjuster used in assessing DV.
- Do not let the insurance company argue that they are under a "permanent injunction" pursuant to the <u>Mabry</u> Order to use 17c. This is BS. First of all,

the Order does not say 17c is the "end all" measure of diminished value. It is a starting point, especially when the insurer receives "relevant information" from it's own insured. Second, the insurance commissioner issued a directive in December of 2008 that required insurers to consider this additional information from it's own insured. State Farm MODIFIED their procedures to consider additional information. Finally, this permanent injunction can not be binding on anyone that was not a member of the settlement class nor had a wreck after the class period *between and including June 30, 1997 and June 20, 2003*.

- In a first party claim, you do not have to hit your demand amount in order to recover for bad faith. For example, if the jury finds bad faith, you will recover 50% of the DV amount in penalties, or $5,000.00 (whichever is greater), plus reasonable attorneys' fees. The law is different in 3rd party claims. With these claims, you must hit your demand amount. For example, if you demanded $2,000.00 in your time limit demand, you must receive at least $2,000.00 in a jury award for DV. If not, you cannot recover bad faith penalties and attorneys' fees.

- You can not send an offer of judgment in a first party claim. The insurance company can not threaten you with one either. Plaintiff's claims are for breach of contract pursuant to **O.C.G.A. Section 33-4-6**. These are not tort claims. (See <u>Estate of Thornton v. Unum Life Ins. Co. of America</u>, 445 F.Supp. 2d 1379 (2006)). **O.C.G.A. Section 9-11-68** only applies to "tort claims".

- You may not seek attorneys' fees under **O.C.G.A. Section 13-6-11**.

IV.   THIRD PARTY DV CLAIMS

A.   Statute:

> **O.C.G.A. Section 33-4-7**   Actions for loss
> under motor vehicle liability policy; insurer's
> liability for bad faith; notice to Commissioner

(a)   In the event of a loss because of injury to or destruction of property covered by a motor vehicle liability insurance policy, the insurer issuing such policy has an   affirmative duty to adjust that loss fairly and promptly, to make a reasonable effort to investigate and evaluate the claim, and, where liability is reasonably clear, to make a good faith effort to settle with the claimant potentially entitled to recover against the insured under such policy. Any insurer who breaches this duty may be liable to pay the claimant, in addition to the loss, not more than 50 percent of the liability of the insured for the loss or $5,000.00, whichever is greater, and all reasonable attorney's fees for the prosecution of the action.

(b)   An insurer breaches the duty of subsection (a) of this Code section when, after   investigation of the claim, liability has become reasonably clear and the insurer in bad faith offers less than the amount reasonably owed under all the circumstances of which the insurer is aware.

(c)   A claimant shall be entitled to recover under subsection (a) of this Code section if the   claimant or the claimant's attorney has delivered to the insurer a demand letter, by statutory overnight delivery or certified mail, return receipt requested, offering to settle for an amount certain; the insurer has refused or declined to do so within 60 days of receipt of such demand, thereby compelling the claimant to institute or continue suit to recover; and the claimant ultimately recovers an amount equal to or in excess of the claimant's demand.

(d)   At the expiration of the 60 days set forth in subsection (c) of this Code section, the   claimant may serve the insurer issuing such policy by service of the complaint in accordance with law. The insurer shall be an unnamed party, not disclosed to the jury, until there has been a verdict resulting in recovery equal to or in excess of the claimant's demand. If that occurs, the trial shall be recommenced in order for the trier of fact to receive evidence to make a determination as to whether bad faith existed in the handling or adjustment of the attempted settlement of the claim or action in question.

(e)   The action for bad faith shall not be abated by payment after the 60 day period nor shall the testimony or opinion of an expert witness be the sole basis for a summary judgment or directed verdict on the issue of bad faith.

(f)   The amount of recovery, including reasonable attorney's fees, if any, shall be determined by the trier of fact and included in a separate judgment against the insurer rendered in the action; provided, however, the attorney's fees shall be fixed on the basis of competent expert evidence as to the reasonable value of the services based on the time spent and legal and factual issues involved in accordance with prevailing fees in the locality where the action is pending; provided, further, the trial court shall have the discretion, if it finds the jury verdict fixing attorney's fees to be greatly excessive or inadequate, to review and amend the portion of the verdict fixing attorney's fees without the necessity of disapproving the entire verdict. The limitations contained in this Code section in reference to the amount of attorney's fees are not controlling as to the fees which may be agreed upon by the plaintiff and his or her attorney for the services of the attorney.

(g)   In any action brought pursuant to subsection (b) of this Code section, and within 20 days of bringing such action, the plaintiff shall, in addition to service of process in accordance with Code Section 9-11-4, mail to the Commissioner of Insurance and the consumers' insurance advocate a copy of the demand and complaint by first-class mail. Failure to comply with this subsection may be cured by delivering same.

HISTORY: Code 1981, Sec. 33-4-7, enacted by Ga. L. 2001, p. 784, Sec. 1.

B.   Nuts and Bolts:

The same rules apply as in first party claims.

- You must send a 60 day Time Limit Demand.
- You can not file your lawsuit until the 60 day time limit demand has expired.
- You still need to support your demand with an appraisal.
- If you file suit, the insurer is an "unnamed party" to the lawsuit. You can still send them discovery.

V.   MABRY and 17c

In paragraph 17 of the Mabry v. State Farm Mutual Automobile Insurance Co. Order on Compliance and Injunction Granting Further and Consistent Relief, dated June 12, 2001, Judge Pullen of the Superior Court of Muscogee County wrote the following:

"Within thirty (30) days of the entry of this Order, State Farm is to submit in writing for approval, by the Court, a methodology for assessment of non-repair related diminished value based on criteria and standards that the Court can approve as being acceptable. State Farm may employ or use the following methodologies to make such required assessments:

(a)   The ClaimCoach.com system;

(b)   The Classic Car Appraisal Service (Don Peterson) methodology;

(c)   The formula distributed by the Georgia Insurance Commissioner's Office and used by Safeco, Progressive, Nationwide, and Crawford & Co.;

(d)   Any combination or modification of (a), (b) or (c) as approved by the Court;

If State Farm were to employ or use (a) or (b) or any combination thereof, such employment and use would be at State Farm's expense."

A lot of insurance companies select 17c as the methodology they use for assessing diminished value. Why? I believe it is simply a business decision. Of all the methodologies, this one consistently generates the lowest amount of diminished value every time. It is also interesting to note that the 17c formula was **NEVER** distributed by the Insurance Commissioner's Office nor approved by the office. It is designed to undercut diminished value payouts for insurers. There is no science behind the methodology.

Here are the basics of the 17c formula:

VEHICLE INFORMATION

Year:
Make:
Model:

NADA SUMMARY		DIMINISHED VALUE SUMMARY	
Base Vehicle:	$_____	NADA Summary x 10% = Base LOV	
Additions:	_____	Base LOV:	$ _____
	_____	Damage Modifier:	$ _____
	_____	Mileage Modifier:	$ _____
	_____	Total Loss of Value:$ _____	
Total:	$ _____		
*Add/Deduct Mileage:			
	$ _____		
TOTAL:	$ _____		

Damage Modifier:

This decision is up to the appraiser. The damage modifier is based on the extent of actual
physical damage sustained by the vehicle, rather than the cost of repair as its basis.

Mileage Modifier:

Mileage:	Modifier:
0 - 19,999	1.0
20,000 - 39,999	.80
40,000 - 59,999	.60
60,000 - 79,999	.40
80,000 - 99,999	.20
100,000 & above	0.00

There are several problems with the 17c formula:

1. It caps the diminished value at 10%. There is no authority that supports the proposition that the most a vehicle can lose in market value due to a wreck and repair is 10%. This is an arbitrary figure. In essence, it is a cap on damages.
2. When the adjuster calculates the NADA base value, he/she takes into account the mileage on the vehicle. But once the base value is calculated, there is another reduction when applying the mileage

modifier. The vehicle's value is getting hit twice with mileage deductions.

3. The damage modifier is another factor that makes zero sense. It does not account for the actual cost of repairs. There is no way one can competently and accurately measure the diminished value of a car without taking into account the dollar amount of the repairs. It does not take into account paint issues; e.g., there is no way to match the factory paint when repairs are made. This is visible to any consumer and will obviously lessen the value of the vehicle. Further, there is no reduction in value under the damage modifier when non-OEM (original equipment of the manufacturer) parts are used.

4. If a vehicle has over 100,000 miles, according to the 17c formula, it effectively sustains ZERO diminished value as the modifier is 0. There is no authority whatsoever in the automobile industry to support this position.

In practice, the carriers that use this formula to assess DV have their claims adjusters do the calculations. If you ever receive a DV "appraisal" that uses the 17c formula, please move to have this excluded. The 17c formula was pre-<u>Daubert</u> and the witness should never be allowed to testify about the formula or the final figure it spits out.

Don't forget the "value" code section: **O.C.G.A. Section 24-9-66**:

> Direct testimony as to market value is in the nature of opinion evidence. One need not be an expert or dealer in the article in question but may testify as to its value if he has had an opportunity for forming a correct opinion.

There is no statutory authority for the 17c methodology. Further, according to case law, there are only two (2) methods for calculating diminished value. <u>Canal Ins. Co. v. Tullis</u>, 237 Ga. App. 515, 516-17(1999), sets the standard: a party seeking to recover for damage to the vehicle has two options in proving the amount of damage. These choices of proof are:

1. The difference between the fair market value of the vehicle before and after the collision; and
2. The reasonable costs of repair, together with hire on the vehicle while rendered incapable of use and the value of any additional permanent impairment, provided that the aggregate of such amounts does not exceed the fair market value before the collision.

See also <u>Myers v. Thornton</u>, supra, <u>Archer v. Monroe</u>, supra; and <u>Sykes v. Sin</u>, supra. The 17c
formula does not fit either one of these methods and should be excluded.

Most claims adjusters can never be qualified as *"experts"* in property damage appraisals.
Most have never been automobile *"dealers."* Some insurers try to get their testimony in
using the 17c claiming they are fact witnesses. Under **O.C.G.A. Section 24-9-66**, the only way
they can testify is to show they have had "an opportunity for forming a correct opinion." 17c
does not allow them to form a correct opinion. It **gives** the adjuster the opinion. The adjuster
at least does a cursory market value survey of the pre-accident value of the vehicle under 17c.
However, there is no post wreck and repair market value survey.

Permanent Injunction Defense:

Do not any insurer argue they are bound by a *"permanent injunction"* pursuant to the March 6, 2002 <u>Mabry</u> Order, and therefore, must use the 17c methodology and nothing more. This is horse manure. The <u>Mabry</u> case was a class action lawsuit that involved a defined class for a specific time period. Judge Pullen did not have any authority to prospectively bind anyone that was not a member of that class. If this were the case, then we need to intervene in every pending class action lawsuit so we might have an opportunity to litigate all of the issues that could bind us in the future.

They will claim that even though your client was not a party to the permanent injunction, they were, and therefore, they must use the formula and only the formula. This makes no sense as the application of this argument effectively binds everyone that was **not** a party to the class action.

Faulty Repairs:

Don't let the insurer argue that "faulty repairs" are the reason for your client's diminished value. This is a separate and distinct claim your client may have against the repair facility. This has nothing to do with your client's "inherent diminished value" claim. For the purposes of this claim, we are assuming the repair facility performed all of the repairs correctly. Even with this being done, the wrecked and repaired vehicle still has diminished value.

CHAPTER 6 – Your Injuries

One of the major elements of a personal injury claim is the medical treatment that our clients undergo for the injuries they sustained in the collision. It is extremely important for any attorney that handles these claims to understand the medical issues. We often will have thousands of pages of medical records for just one seriously injured client. It is our job to sift through these records to create a medical history and summary of treatment so we can present the most accurate picture possible to the insurance company about our client's injuries, surgeries, physical therapy, and prescription medications. We also need to have a strong understanding of our client's injuries and treatment so we can intelligently discuss this with the treating physicians - either in face-to-face conferences or in depositions.

Most attorneys have never gone to medical school or had any formal medical training. This is still NO excuse for the attorney, as he/she needs to gain a greater understanding of medical terms and procedures. If necessary, we hire doctors or nurse consultants to help us evaluate the medical information so we can put it into a format that a layman can understand.

In this chapter, we will break down a typical medical record, and put in layman's language some of the common terms we see in patient's charts. We will also provide a list of some of the diagnostic tools treating physicians use to evaluate injuries, and then conclude with various types of treatment prescribed. This is by no means an exhaustive list, however. If you have any questions regarding the facts of your medical diagnosis or treatment, you are encouraged to discuss this with your treating physician and your personal injury attorney.

Medical Records:

Doctors typically use what is referred to as a "S.O.A.P." system when memorializing notes of a patient visit. The acronym S.O.A.P. stands for:

- Subjective
- Objective
- Assessment and
- Plan

Each of these elements is explained below:

Subjective:

This is the section that lists the patient's major complaints. The nurse and/or the doctor will take a history from the patient as to WHY they are seeing the doctor. The history can include:

- Past medical history
- Any diseases
- Any issues for which they are under a doctor's care, such as diabetes, high blood pressure, cancer, etc.
- Surgical history
- Any current medications
- Any allergies
- And then the note will deal with the HPI - or history of present illness.

HPI: This is the reason why you are treating with the doctor. We encourage all of our clients to be as thorough as possible when explaining to the doctor their complaints of pain. Remember: not all injuries are visible. Not all injuries will produce swelling. Sometimes injuries cannot be seen with the naked eye. The only way the nurse or doctor can diagnose these injuries is to be told about the complaints of pain so further testing may be performed. This is NOT whining!

We always tell our clients that they need to start from the top of their head and go to the tip of their toes to tell the medical professionals about their injuries. If a part of your body was injured and only hurt for a brief period, it is still important to tell the doctor so this can be memorialized in the physician's or chiropractor's notes.

Imagine this scenario:

> You are involved in a rear-end collision. The defendant pick up truck smashes into the rear of your car and totals it. Your neck is injured, and you have pain in your right shoulder that shoots down your right arm. You are taken to the emergency room by ambulance and the EMT's have you immobilized on a back board so you can not move around and possibly aggravate the neck injury. An MRI is performed on your neck (cervical MRI), and thankfully the test does not show any kind of bulging or herniated disk. The doctors were obviously concerned about your neck injury, and were also relieved when the tests came back normal. However, in all of the excitement and worry about your neck, you never mentioned your right shoulder or arm. You just assume it will get better, and the problem with your upper extremity is really due to your neck hurting. When you go to your doctor, even though the right shoulder and arm still hurt, you do not mention it to him and he focuses solely on the neck.

> Many weeks go by and the right shoulder and arm become more of a problem and not just a nagging injury. You go to the doctor and he sends you to have an MRI of the right upper extremity. The radiologist reviews the MRI scans and finds a rotator cuff tear. You had never injured this shoulder before and you now believe that the tear happened when you were bracing against the steering wheel at impact. But now that months have gone by without any mention of the right shoulder injury in any of your medical notes, the insurance company is refusing to consider the right shoulder issues as a part of their claim. So you must fight them to get them to accept the injury.

These problems could have more than likely been prevented if you had mentioned the right shoulder and right arm pain to the doctor from the very beginning.

Again, we recommend telling the nurse / doctor:

- when the pain started;
- where the pain is located;
- they type of pain (dull, achy, shooting, burning)
- tell the doctor if the pain is confined to one area, or does it radiate down your arms or legs?
- what helps alleviate the pain? What makes it go away or better?
- how often do you have the pain?
- do you have any other symptoms when the pain is present?

It may help you to make a list of your injuries / pains if you tend to forget. Sometimes, nurses and doctors will try to rush through this time. Make sure you have their full attention and ask them to please document these injuries and complaints of pain.

Objective:

This is the examination and testing portion of the visit. The medical chart could list some of the following:

- your vital signs, such as blood pressure and temperature.
- a record of the physical examination that the doctor performs.
- results from any blood work, x-rays, CT scans, MRI scans, nerve conduction studies, or other diagnostic tests.

Assessment:

Based upon the subjective information and the objective testing, the doctor will record his assessment of your condition, i.e., his diagnosis. He will write a quick summary as to what he thinks the problem(s) are and normally put it in an order from most likely problem to least likely but possible problem.

Plan:

This is the final part of the medical note. This is a list of what the doctor plans to do to further diagnose and/or treat the problem(s). The plan could include:

- an Order for testing, such as more blood work or diagnostic scans like an x-ray, CT scan, or MRI.
- a referral for physical therapy or chiropractic treatment.
- -prescriptions such as pain medication or anti-inflammatories.
- a referral to a specialist, such as an orthopedic surgeon or neurosurgeon.
- a schedule for surgery.
- the patient may also be given written educational information regarding their injury and a suggested course of treatment at home.
- follow up appointments, if any, will be noted here as well.

Most Common Injuries:

Every wreck is different - not only in how it happens, but how the impact of the collision effects the occupants of the vehicle (or the person on the motorcycle). A rear end collision that only leaves a small bumper crack may be enough force to cause severe injuries to someone that was medically fragile to start. Please do not believe for one second some of the insurance propaganda that is disseminated that tries to support the proposition that no one can be injured in a low impact, minor property damage claim.

In this section, we will list the most typical injuries we see in car wreck claims:

Soft Tissue:

Most medical journals define soft tissue as the extra-skeletal tissue of the body, including the muscles, your fat and fibrous tissues, your blood vessels, and the peripheral nerves contained in the tissues. We typically refer to the soft tissue as the muscles, tendons and ligaments that connect to and help support our body structure. Whenever the soft tissue is injured, it usually results in a strain, sprain, contusion, laceration or amputation.

In a lot of rear-end collisions, our clients sustain injuries to the neck and the back when they are thrown forward, stopped, and then move backward rapidly. These are often referred to as "whiplash" injuries. This sudden acceleration/deceleration results in a tearing or stretching of the soft tissue. The injuries can be incredibly painful, debilitating, and annoying. The patient will often experience pain, swelling, bruising, or loss of range of motion or function from these injuries. Common symptoms include nausea, headaches, and stiffness and pain whenever someone tries to move their neck or back.

Treatment for these injuries by doctors, chiropractors, or physical therapists often uses some form of the RICE principle. **RICE** stands for:

> **R**est: Take it easy! The patient is to avoid doing any activity that causes pain or could re-aggravate the injury.

> **I**ce: It is extremely important to apply ice to the injured area during the first 72 hours after an injury. This will help minimize pain and control some swelling at the site.

> **C**ompression: The patient should apply pressure to the injured area by using a bandage or some kind of sports wrap to help reduce the swelling.

> **E**levation: The patient is encouraged to keep the injured part of their body above the level of their heart as much as they can tolerate during the first 72 hours.

Please note: The insurance company is quick to try and attack these injuries since they are not visible to the naked eye, nor can they be seen on x-rays or other diagnostic scans. Because of this, the adjusters will claim that the patient is sometimes "exaggerating" or "faking" their symptoms. They know that it is often difficult to demonstrate these injuries to a jury so they make very small offers - especially if the cars involved in the wreck did not have a lot of property damage.

Fractures:

A fracture is medical terminology for a broken bone. There are different types of fractures, though:

Displaced: This is when the bone is broken into two or more parts and the bones have moved so the ends are no longer aligned.

Non-displaced: The bone is broken either part of the way or completely, but the ends have not moved and the bones are still in proper alignment.

Open: This is where the broken bone actually penetrates through the skin.

Closed: The bone has been broken, but there is no open wound or penetration through the skin.

When doctors analyze the severity of a fracture, they look to see how much damage was done to the bone as well as to the surrounding tissue. In addition, if it is an open fracture, there are a lot of worries about the potential of infection. Other complications from a broken bone could include damage to blood vessels or the nerves.

Immediate first aid for the fracture depends on its severity and the location. The most important component is immobilizing the broken bone - preventing it from being moved. This is often done with a splint.

Treatment options may include:

- casting of the bone once it is aligned;
- surgical intervention. This may involve an internal or external fixation device which uses hardware like pins, plates, rods or screws.
- sometimes the location of the fracture prevents aggressive treatment. For example, a broken rib can be treated at home with ice and rest.

Disk Injuries:

The spinal column (also called the vertebral column) consists of a series of bones (vertebrae) that are stacked one upon another. The spine consists of 33 vertebrae - 24 of which are called "articulating" vertebrae which are separated by intervertebral discs, and 9 fused vertebrae in the sacrum and coccyx.

The spine is divided into four (4) sections:

1. Cervical   (neck)
2. Thoracic   (upper back / chest)
3. Lumbar   (lower back)
4. Sacral   (pelvic region)

Each sections has the following number of vertebrae:

- Cervical   7
- Thoracic   12
- Lumbar   5
- Sacrum   5
- Coccygeal   4

Each of the vertebrae in the cervical, thoracic and lumbar region are separated and cushioned by an intervertebral disk. This disc acts like a cushion and helps keep the vertebrae from rubbing together. These disks are held in place by ligaments that connect the spinal bones and the surrounding muscle sheaths. Inside the disk is a jelly-like substance known as the nucleus, or nucleus pulposus. This disk and the nucleus inside act as shock absorbers for the spine and are able to adjust to various types of movement and weight on the spine. In children, these disks are gel or fluid filled sacs. By adulthood, the blood supply going to the disk has greatly decreased and the soft gel starts to harden. In your middle age, the disks are very tough and have lost their elasticity. These changes as you age make your disks more prone to injury.

We have handled thousands of cases for individuals with disk problems that were either caused or aggravated from car wrecks or on the job injuries. The pain that these people experienced was excruciating. You could just see it in their faces and in their general demeanor. Every movement they would make would cause pain and it was difficult for them to find a position that did not exacerbate their condition. But as many doctors and surgeons have told us, this pain is a warning sign to the person that they have a major medical problem that needs correction. The pain can be sharp or shooting, or sometimes dull and achy. Other symptoms could include numbness, tingling, a weakness in the muscle, or even paralysis.

A spinal disk bulge or herniation can be caused by trauma, lifting, and sometimes degenerative changes. For example, the force of the collision will cause a tear in the outer part of the disk, the annulus fibrosus, which allows the nucleus to bulge out of the ring. This tear allows that protruding disk to sometimes press against surrounding nerves causing debilitating pain and discomfort.

Disk problems can sometimes be treated temporarily with anti-inflammatory medications, as well as muscle relaxers and pain killers. More aggressive therapies could include epidural steriod injections. A lot of times this is just a short term relieving of the symptoms and not a long term solution to the problem. Surgical intervention is generally considered a last resort or if there is a concern of paralysis or other significant neurological deficit.

Some of the more common surgical options include:

- Discectomy
- Fusion

- Laminectomy
- Hemilaminectomy

The length of the time that a patient takes to recover greatly depends on the severity of the injury, the overall health of the patient, the age of the patient, and how much pain they can tolerate through the rehabilitation process.

Other Injuries:

Over the years, we have practically seen every imaginable type of injury in our practice. Below is a list of other types of injuries we have handled, but it is by no means exhaustive:

- Closed head injuries
- Paralysis claims
- Concussions
- Crush injuries
- Amputations
- Avulsion fractures
- Penetration wounds
- Significant Burns
- Blunt trauma
- Injuries caused by chemical burns
- Scarring and keloid scarring
- Carpal tunnel
- Rotator cuff injuries
- Collapsed lungs
- Fractured hips
- Torn ACL and MCL injuries

and non-motor vehicle injuries, including:

- Rapes and sexual assaults
- Shootings
- Stabbings
- Dog bites
- Chemical burns

- Other burn injuries
- Carpal tunnel

And over the years, we have handled many death claims that have been caused by car wrecks, on the job injuries, or due to inadequate security at commercial establishments.

Diagnostic Tests

There are various diagnostic tests that doctors can use to diagnose a patient's condition, as well as to evaluate the seriousness of the problems. In this section, I'll break the tests into two categories based upon who performs the tests:

1. Machine
2. Doctor

Tests Performed by Machine:

(1)   x-rays:

This is a machine that emits a type of electromagnetic radiation. The machine sends these particles through your body and the images are recorded onto a computer or a film. The test is painless and you cannot feel any of the radiation passing through your body. A radiologist will review the images and write a report of his/her findings. X-rays are used to diagnose fractures, dislocations, some degenerative joint diseases, and internal trauma.

(2)   MRI (Magnetic Resonance Imaging):

An MRI machine uses powerful magnets and radio waves instead of radiation to help physicians get an inside look at your body. It is also a painless test. MRI's can sometimes allow physicians to see things in a scan that will not be revealed in an x-ray or CT scan. The test is often prescribed to find problems such as bleeding, tumors, tears, blood vessel diseases, or injuries. It is often used to detect bleeding in the brain from trauma, viewing torn ligaments or tendons in the shoulders or knees, or for the doctor to check the disks and nerves of the spine for disk herniations.

(3)   CT Scan (Computerized Axial Tomography):

These are special types of x-rays taken with the assistance of a computer to allow the technician to scan different views and cross sections of your body. It produces a scan with much higher definition and resolution than a standard x-ray. The pictures can show if there is any bleeding on the brain or other internal injuries, fractures, or nerve impingement.

(4)   Ultrasound:

This is a machine that uses ultrasound (high frequency) waves to detect any kind of structural or functional abnormalities in the body. Since the machine is showing the images in real time, the technician can record it or the doctor can view it live to see how the body's internal organs are functioning, or the blood flowing through blood vessels. This test allows physicians to evaluate symptoms such as swelling, pain, or infection.

(5)   EEG (Electroencephalogram):

This is a test that will measure and record any electrical activity in the patient's brain. The technician will place special sensors called electrodes to the patient's head and the wires go to a computer to analyze and record the data. The test may be used to find out if a comatose patient is "brain-dead" or if there is some activity occurring. It is also used after a head injury to see if seizure activity is present.

(6)   ICP (Intracranial Pressure Monitoring):

When ICP is performed, a medical device is implanted inside the head to detect the pressure inside the skull. The data is sent to a recording device for the physician to review.

Some Tests performed by Doctors during exams:

(1)   Straight Leg Raising Test:

This may be abbreviated in the notes as "SLR." The test is performed to help diagnose a herniated disk in the lower back. The patient is instructed to lie on his back. While on the table, the patient's legs are lifted while the knee is kept straight. If the patient complains of pain while the leg is between 30 degrees and 70 degrees, then the test is considered positive and the patient has a likely diagnosis of a herniated disk.

(2)   Naffziger's Test:

In this test, the patient is seated and the examiner stands behind her and applies pressure to the jugular veins for approximately 40 - 45 seconds. This pressure prevents blood from flowing from the head while the heart continues to pump blood into the head. The test is positive if it shows an increase or an aggravation of the pain. This could indicate a nerve-root compression by a intervertebral disk.

(3)   Spurling's Test:

This is a test used to check for cervical radiculopathy (a pinched nerve in the neck). The patient is seated and the examiner turns the patient's head from side to side and applies downward pressure to the top of the head. If pain radiates from the patient's neck down the upper extremity/ arm, then the test is positive.

(4)   Bragard's Sign:

This is a test between muscle pain or disk problems in the lower back. The patient lies down and the doctor will left the leg on the side where the patient indicates he is hurting until the patient starts to complain of pain. The doctor will then bend the foot on that side backwards. If the patient complains of an increase in the pain while the foot is bent, then the test is positive.

(5)   Femoral Nerve Stretch:

This test is used to detect disk problems in the lower back - mainly between the third and fourth lumbar verterbrae. The patient is lying down on the exam table on his stomach. The doctor grabs the foot on one of the legs and bends the leg back towards the buttocks while trying to keep the thigh flat against the table. The test is positive if it produces pain in the lower back or in the thigh.

(6)   Bakody Sign:

This is a test to determine if there is some nerve root impingement in the neck region - typically between C4 and C6 vertebrae. While sitting, the patient is asked to place the palm of their hand on top of their head. If there is a decrease in pain, the test is considered positive.

There are so many other tests that are used by doctors and chiropractors - far more than are covered here. Some doctors may choose not to use any of these tests depending upon the results of the diagnostic scans. We strongly encourage you to discuss the findings of these tests with your treating physician and your attorney.

CHAPTER 7 – Medical Treatment for Your Injuries

If you have been injured in a car wreck, it is important that you get prompt medical care for your injuries. This should be done regardless of whether or not you plan on ever presenting any kind of claim against the at fault party's insurance company. You had your health before the wreck and you need to get that back as best you can. This should be your ultimate goal.

The following guidelines should help you as you treat for your injuries:

Describe All Of Your Injuries

It is extremely important that you tell the nurse or doctor about all of your injuries, even if something only hurts a little.

Three reasons for full disclosure:

1. The doctor will not be able to treat an injury he/she does not know about so be as descriptive as possible. All injuries are not visible - such as strains and sprains or internal injuries. Do not rely on them to discover all injuries based upon their examination. This is also not a time to play it tough. If you hurt, tell the doctor.
2. If you do not tell the doctor about an injury because you think it is minor and will get better, but a few weeks later the condition worsens, you are going to have some potential problems. It may be more difficult for the doctor to treat your condition because of the delay. From a legal standpoint, the insurance company may not consider this "injury" as being related to the car wreck because there was no previous mention of it to your doctor. The insurer could allege you hurt yourself somewhere else at some other time and are now trying to wrongly place responsibility on them.

3. If you describe all of your injuries, the medical professionals will document them in their records. These medical records are an integral part of the demand package which will be sent to the insurance adjuster when it is time to settle your claim. These records will memorialize all of your injuries, tests, prescriptions, and treatments that were provided to you by the health care professional.

Do Not Delay Seeking Medical Treatment

If you are hurt, go to the doctor! It is important for you to be examined by a medical professional if you are injured in a wreck - even if you do not plan on pursuing a personal injury claim. People often will leave the scene of a wreck feeling they are not injured - just a little sore. But when they wake up the next day, the pain, the tightness or soreness in the muscles hit them like a ton of bricks. If this happens to you, I encourage you to seek immediate medical attention.

Medical Treatment And Your Personal Injury Claim:

It is important to keep in mind that major components of your personal injury claim are the nature of your injuries and the medical treatment you receive for these injuries! If you do not tell the nurse or doctor about an injury, chances are it will never make it into your medical records. If you later try and allege these injuries are related, you will have no proof or documentation to support your claims and the insurance company will not consider it when evaluating your case.

When treating with any health care professional for the injuries sustained in the wreck, you should:

- Tell each one about ALL of your injuries.
- Keep ALL medical appointments. If you do not go, the insurance company will penalize you when assigning a settlement value to your claim. The adjuster knows that judges and juries will not be understanding of missed

appointments - UNLESS there is a legitimate reason for you not going.

- Comply with the doctor's treatment recommendations. If they tell you to go to therapy 3 times a week, then go 3 times a week. If you are prescribed home exercises, then do them. First, you should do this as this will more than likely help you get better. Second, if you only go 2 times a week when 3 is recommended, the insurance adjuster will minimize your injuries. They will claim that if you were "really" hurt, you would have been compliant.

- If you cannot make an appointment, please call the doctor's office before the appointment out of courtesy to them. It is also important to let them know if you can't make it because you are hurting too bad or you can not drive because the medication impairs your ability to operate a motor vehicle. This will allow the doctor's office to document the reason why you could not make it. The doctor will also not note in your medical records that you were a "no show."

- Let each doctor know about other medical facilities or practitioners you have seen for your injuries, as well as what tests, treatments, and prescriptions have been given to you.

- It is also important for you to go to the doctor for a final "discharge" visit. This will allow the doctor to summarize all of your injuries, the treatment provided to you, and the likelihood that you will need future treatment, therapy, prescriptions, or possibly even surgery for those problems. The doctor can also render an opinion as to whether or not your injuries are permanent.

Document Your Injuries

We have all heard the expression "A picture is worth a thousand words." You can describe to someone all day long the "horrific gash" on your forehead because of the crash. There is another expression we need to keep in mind though - "The easiest pain to bear is someone else's." Nothing illustrates your injury more than a photograph - showing the injury at its worse. Words can go in one ear and out the other but a picture of the injury can make an indelible mark on a jury.

Whenever possible and when necessary, we have professional photographs taken of our clients' injuries. A properly trained evidence photographer can help memorialize the visible injuries. They will use tools like a ruler in the picture to give the viewer a frame of reference - to understand the length of the scar or the size of the metal brace protruding out of the skin with screws and plates to keep the fractured bone in place so it can heal properly. It is worth the time, effort and money.

Is The Injury Causally Related To The Wreck?

If you are involved in a wreck, you may sustain injuries that you might not be able to directly link to the wreck. For example, you start having pain in your wrists a week or two after the accident. You may not realize that you have a carpal tunnel injury because you were gripping the steering wheel tightly at the instant of impact. Or your knee may start hurting a few days after the wreck. You do not remember it hitting anything inside the car so you are not sure if it is related. Make sure you tell your doctor about the injury and give some thought as to why it may be hurting. With your knee, did you brace your leg against the floorboard immediately prior to the crash? It is important for you to know that not all injuries are caused by direct contact with something in your vehicle.

Does The Injury Prevent You From Working?

If you are not able to work because of your injuries, and you want to seek reimbursement for your lost wages in your personal injury claim, it is crucial to get a doctor's disability slip taking you out of work. Juries can understand a person with a back injury not being able to perform their job as a landscaper. They may not understand how a fractured ankle could keep a telephone receptionist from working, however. Make sure the doctor knows the type of work you do and whether or not you feel you can do the job with the restrictions he places on you because of your injuries.

Make sure the disability slip is for a specific period of time. If it is set to expire when you see the doctor at the next follow-up appointment and you are still disabled, get another disability slip for a new time period. If you must turn these in to your employer, make a copy of the slip for your attorney and yourself. These disability slips will help document your lost wage claim in your demand package.

One caveat: even though your doctor tells you that you should be disabled from work, it does not necessarily mean your employer agrees or has to abide by it. If you do not show up for work because of injuries sustained in a wreck, some states will allow your employer to fire you - even with a valid disability from a medical doctor. You should ask yourself these questions: how important is this job to you? Can you "tough it out" and do your job without re-injuring yourself or aggravating your injuries? Do your injuries present a safety risk to you - or other workers? When your health improves and you are capable of returning to gainful employment, will it be easy for you to find a new job if you are fired from your current one? These are questions to which only you know the answer.

Do Not Go To The Doctor To "Run Up" Your Medical Bills

Please do not think that the greater the amount of your medical bills, the larger your settlement with the insurance company will be! The insurance company - as well as judges and juries - will only consider medical bills that are reasonable and necessary. Do not go to the doctor just to go to the doctor to increase your medical bills. Go to the doctor because you are hurting and need treatment.

If a chiropractor or doctor tells you that you need to come in so many times a week for a number of weeks so you can get to a certain dollar threshold for your medical bills, please let your attorney know this! We want the doctor to worry about you recovering for your injuries. We take care of getting the recovery on the personal injury settlement.

It is up to you to make sure you understand the treatment plan that the doctor is prescribing for you. If you have questions, ask him or her. If tests are recommended, ask the doctor to describe the test for you and find out the reason for the test. We are always available to discuss our client's treatment plan with them and to address their concerns about the kind of care and attention they are being provided by their doctor.

What Happens If You Are Not Getting Better?

Assume you have been compliant with all of your doctor's instructions. You have faithfully gone to physical therapy, you've done the recommended home exercises, and you took the prescription medications as indicated. But you still hurt and you do not feel you are getting better. What next?

We encourage you to schedule an appointment with your doctor to discuss your medical care and treatment plan. Some additional testing may be necessary. The doctor may need to refer you out to a specialist to address your specific medical problems.

Here are two things that do not need to happen:

1. You just assume the problems are not going to get better and you just deal with it.
2. You should not allow the doctor to tell you "I don't know what else to do" if you feel he has not done everything possible. If this happens, you may want to seriously consider going for a second opinion.

> One word of warning: You are the one that is hurting. You have every right to try and find the best possible medical care for your injuries, even if it means going to more than one doctor. But we highly recommend you don't jump from one doctor to the next

unless you have been fully compliant with the doctors and completed the treatment plans they have recommended. Failure to follow their prescriptions could be considered "doctor shopping" by the insurance company!

Keep Track Of ALL Medical Doctors and Medical Bills

We encourage our clients to keep a list of all the medical doctors that they see for treatment for their injuries. Whenever they go to a doctor's office for the first time, we ask them to grab a business card from that doctor and immediately send it to us. This way we can keep track of all of the doctors, as well as the office location that the client attended. When our client completes their medical treatment, we will have a complete and accurate list of all of their doctors so we can order all of their medical records from these providers.

Please keep ALL medical bills and invoices you receive from these facilities - whether they are handed to you at the doctor's office or mailed to you. In addition, keep ALL instructions the doctor or nurse gives you each visit. This could include any discharge instructions, home exercise charts, or referrals to other physicians. ALL of this material is extremely important to your claim - especially in the presentation of a demand package to the insurance company.

CHAPTER 8 – Who Pays Your Medical Bills

So you were injured in a car wreck and it was not your fault. Because of your injuries, you are taken by ambulance to the emergency room where you are examined by ER physicians, many diagnostic tests are performed, including x-rays and a CT Scan. You are discharged with several prescriptions and instructions to follow up with a medical doctor due to the nature and extent of the injuries.

It seems as though as soon as you arrive home, pull into the driveway, and walk to the mailbox, you open it up to find bills from the hospital, the emergency room physician, the diagnostic imaging center, and the radiologist. These bills total thousands of dollars. And you still need to see another doctor and get more medical treatment.

Who pays for these medical bills? What are your options? These are questions we receive from our clients every day and I am sure you share the same concerns. The questions can certainly get complicated as personal injury claims can take some time to get resolved. We do everything possible to quickly explore all options available to our clients so we can get their bills paid promptly.

The following information will provide you with a general overview. However, I encourage you to speak with an experienced personal injury attorney regarding the specific facts of your case to investigate and determine all sources of recovery for payment of your medical bills, as well as other items of loss or damage.

Here are some important facts you need to know:

(1)   **At Fault Party's Insurance Company**:

The insurance company for the driver that caused the wreck (the liability carrier) will rarely ever pay for any of your medical bills as you incur them. Please do not think you simply mail the insurer the medical bills and they will pay them. This will not happen.

When you have finished treating and have collected all of your bills, the insurance company will evaluate your claim for settlement. Assuming you do not have an attorney and your case settles, the insurance company will send you one check and you agree to pay for all medical bills. If there is a valid hospital lien filed against your personal injury recovery, the liability insurer may send a check directly to the hospital for the lien amount, or include the hospital as a joint payee on the settlement check. If the settlement does not cover all of your medical bills, these bills are still your responsibility.

There is one other thing I want to stress about the liability carrier and your medical bills. Insurance companies do not bend over backwards to accept your medical bills as "reasonable and necessary." They just are not built this way as they are "for profit" businesses. They will argue that your medical bills are inflated, unnecessary, and unreasonable. The adjuster will claim you treated too long with the doctor, went to too many therapy sessions, and took too many pills because you were simply trying to inflate your medical bills to increase your settlement. If you want to try and take on the insurance company and their lawyers - and allow *them* to decide what medical treatment and bills were "reasonably and necessary", then go ahead. I would strongly suggest you speak with an attorney, however.

(2)   **Your Insurance Company:**

Please pull out a copy of your automobile insurance policy. Find the "Declarations Of Coverage" page ("Dec Page"). This will provide you with a summary of the insurance coverage you have on your vehicle(s). If you don't have a copy of the Dec Page, then call your insurance agent as soon as possible and have him send you a copy. You will want to scan your policy to see if you have Medical Payments Coverage or "MPC." This type of coverage is like a health insurance policy for any occupants involved in a car wreck in your vehicle - regardless of who is at fault. The insurance company will pay for "reasonable and necessary" medical expenses up to the limits of the policy. If the insurer pays the providers under your Med Pay coverage, you typically do not have to repay this money back. There are some conditions where the Med Pay carrier may claim a right to be reimbursed if they can prove you have been "made whole", or fully and completely compensated for your injuries.

This is yet another time when an attorney should be consulted and hired to step in and protect you. In fact, insurance companies tick me off when they ask to be repaid in situations such as this. They have been charging your premiums based upon this contingency happening; i.e., that they might have to pay your medical bills. When it does happen, they should not get a penny in return. Do you think they would ever refund you any of your premiums if you never used it?

If you do not have Med Pac coverage, I highly suggest you immediately call your insurance agent and do two things:

1. Ask him or her why they never suggested you purchase this coverage before the wreck happened. If they are really looking after your best interest, this coverage would have been highly recommended to you (along with uninsured/underinsured motorists' coverage). MPC is not expensive and it provides tangible benefits to you and anyone riding in your car. It is especially important if you do not have health insurance!

2. Purchase MPC and add it immediately to your policy so you and all your passengers will be protected. A suggested amount could be anywhere between $2,500.00 and $5,000.00 of coverage. However, this is a discussion for you and your agent based upon a lot of different factors not covered here.

If you have MPC, then we suggest you use it wisely. Your first concern should be to pay the bills incurred at the hospital. The hospital is less likely to work with you on paying off your bill if you have a limited recovery. Also, the hospital can place a lien on any personal injury recovery so their bill is not one to be ignored.

Some chiropractors and medical doctors will ask you on the first visit to their office if you have med pay coverage. Don't get me wrong - these health care providers have every right to be paid for reasonable and necessary medical services rendered to their patients and they should know about all sources of available payment to them. But over the years, we have seen some of the unscrupulous ones quickly amass a $1,500.00 bill on the patient's first visit to try and get as much of the MPC as possible before it is exhausted. So before you agree for any chiropractor or doctor to treat you, make sure you know in advance what their charges will be for all of their services.

(3)   <u>Workers' Compensation:</u>

In Georgia, if you are involved in a wreck that happened while you were "in the course and scope of your employment" and your employer has three or more employees, there is a strong likelihood that your medical bills can be paid through workers' compensation insurance through your employer. If you were injured while on a lunch break or running a personal errand, chances are workers' compensation coverage will not apply.

It is important to note that you do not have to actually be at a work site to be covered under workers' compensation in Georgia. If your job requires you to drive around for the benefit of the employer and you are injured in collision, I highly recommend that you contact an experienced personal injury and workers' compensation attorney to help you file your claim.

What happens if you are driving in to work and you are in a crash - or you are in one on the way home? Injuries traveling to and from work are typically not considered on the job injuries and, therefore, are not covered by workers' compensation. But there are exceptions to every rule so the best course of conduct is to contact an attorney to discuss the specific facts of your claim.

(4) **Health Insurance**:

If you have health insurance, make sure that you are persistent in getting ALL of your health care providers to bill your health insurer. They may try and tell you that your health insurer will not pay your bills. THIS IS FALSE. Provided your doctor accepts your health insurance and you have complied with the terms of the policy, your health insurer cannot reject your claim because it was a car wreck. (An exception to this is if the accident happened while on the job. Workers' Compensation coverage would apply).

Follow up with all of your carriers to make sure they have your health insurance information AND that they have billed your health insurer. Some hospitals will HOLD medical bills instead of submitting them to health insurance if they know you have a potential personal injury claim. Why? Because the hospital enters into a contract with the health insurer where they agree to a reduced rate for their bills. For example, the regular price for one x-ray might be $250.00. However, the hospital agrees to reduce the bill to $40 for the health insurer. If the hospital puts a "lien" on your personal injury recovery, they will claim a right to be paid the full $250.00, not the $40 negotiated health insurance amount.

If your health insurer pays for the bills you incur because of a car wreck, they may also put a "lien" on your personal injury recovery. In some situations, the health insurer may have a right to be reimbursed. The only way to determine whether or not the health insurer must be repaid out of the recovery is to have an attorney review the health insurance plan language. If the plan is guaranteed a right of recovery, we often get the insurer to reduce the amount of their lien substantially.

Another reason to use your health insurance is to help prevent your medical bills from going to a collection agency. This could certainly have a negative effect on your credit. Also, the doctor's office may not be willing to treat you in the future if you have health insurance and you do not allow them to bill it.

Any time you go to any health care provider for treatment of the injuries you sustained in the car wreck, please make sure you give them your insurance information. Please find on the next page a flow chart to determine the order in which the insurers are responsible:

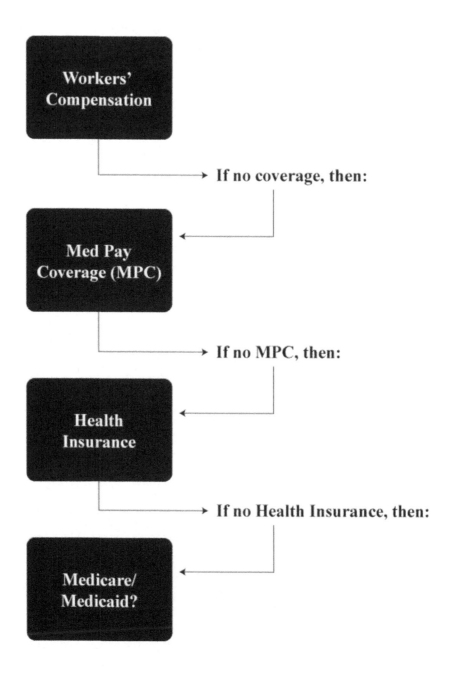

If no other source of insurance, then your best bet if you need continuing treatment is to work with an attorney to help find a doctor who is willing to treat you on a "lien" basis.

CHAPTER 9 – The 3 Things You Must Prove To Recover Damages In Your Car Wreck Claim

Whenever a potential client calls my firm for their free confidential consultation regarding their car wreck, I stress to them that there are 3 things we must prove for them to be successful in their car wreck claims. We have to establish:

1. Someone was negligent in causing the wreck;
2. Prove that the person's negligence was the proximate cause of their injuries;
3. Show the injuries and damages that were sustained as a result of the wreck.

This may sound somewhat complicated, but let me break down each of these 3 elements below:

(1)   <u>Negligence:</u>

We have to prove that someone (besides yourself) was at fault for causing the wreck. This is often referred to as "negligence." Negligence is the failure to exercise reasonable or ordinary care in the operation of their vehicle. This means the care that a "reasonable person" would have exercised or used in the same circumstances. The injured party has the burden of proof in showing that the Defendant driver was negligent in causing the wreck.

For example:

The Defendant has a duty or obligation to do something, and they do it in an unsafe and negligent manner.

- When the defendant rear-ends your car because they were not exercising reasonable care as they did not maintain a safe following distance or failed to keep a proper lookout of the road ahead, they were negligent.

The Defendant has a duty or obligation to do something, and they completely fail to do it.

Georgia law requires the Defendant to keep his vehicle in good, safe working condition if he is going to operate it on the public roads.

- When the defendant rear-ends your car because he did not get his brakes repaired, even though he knew they were not working properly, he is negligent.

We may establish that the Defendant was negligent because he violated a Federal or state statute. For example:

Georgia law prohibits a driver from running through a stop sign. All drivers must come to a complete stop and yield the right of way to other vehicles in the intersection before proceeding. **O.C.G.A. Section 40-6-72(b)**. If the Defendant does not stop and drives through a stop sign into the intersection and crashes into your vehicle, then he is negligent. (Keep in mind: not everyone out there will be honest and admit they did this so there still may have to be proof of this traffic violation in court).

Other examples could include:

- Failure to keep a proper lookout
- Following too closely
- Driver distractions due to using a cell phone or adjusting the radio
- Speeding or traveling too fast for conditions
- Tailgating
- Driving under the influence of alcohol or some illegal drug
- Failure to yield while turning left
- Driver fatigue because they drove their tractor trailer more than Federal law allows

There may be times where we need to hire an expert to help us prove the Defendant was negligent. For example:

Georgia law imposes speed limits on vehicles. We may need to hire an accident reconstructionist to examine the scene of the wreck and the vehicles involved to determine whether or not speed played a role in causing the collision.

(2)   <u>Proximate Cause</u>:

Once we prove the other driver was negligent, then we must show that the negligence was the proximate cause of your injuries. I know this sounds somewhat confusing. How could their negligence NOT cause my injuries? Here is an example:

- Assume that the other driver is under the influence of alcohol when he is operating his car. He is stopped at the red light and you run into the rear of his car. You are seriously injured.

The Defendant should NOT have been operating his vehicle while he was drunk. Clearly, no reasonable person would have done what he did. However, the fact that he was negligent in the operation of his car while he was under the influence of alcohol DID NOT CAUSE the wreck. Your failure to keep a proper lookout caused you to have the collision. Therefore, his negligence was not the proximate cause of the wreck nor your injuries.

These are some clear examples where the wreck was proximately caused by the defendant driver:

- You are at a complete stop at a red light and the Defendant is not paying attention to the road ahead and crashes into the rear of your car.
- You have a green light allowing you to proceed straight through the intersection. The Defendant is traveling in the opposite direction. He does not see you and he attempts to turn left in front of your car and crashes into your vehicle. His failure to yield while turning left is the cause of the collision.

There may be a situation where the Defendant will try and place some blame on you for causing the wreck. This is known as contributory negligence. He may claim that the wreck would not have occurred if you were not at fault as well for causing the collision. If the Defendant is able to show some negligence on your part, the judge and jury can reduce your recovery proportionately.

(3) Damages:

When we prove that the Defendant was negligent and his negligence was the proximate cause of the wreck, we must now prove what damages were inflicted upon you. There are a variety of different types of damages you can potentially recover in your car wreck claim.

Georgia law addresses the issue of damages in the following statute:

> **O.C.G.A. Section 51-12-4**: "Damages are given as compensation for injury; generally, such compensation is the measure of damages where an injury is of a character capable of being estimated in money. If an injury is small or the mitigating circumstances are strong, nominal damages only are given."

So damages are measured in money. Whenever we make a claim for money damages, we have the burden of proving the amount of the loss to a degree where the judge or jury can calculate the amount of the loss to a reasonable degree of certainty. The amount rendered in a verdict is to "compensate" the plaintiff for their damages. It is the law's way of making them whole again.

Georgia law recognizes that there are two types of compensatory damages, "general" and "special." These are set forth in the following statute:

O.C.G.A. Section 51-12-2:

"(a) General damages are those which the law presumes to flow from any tortious act; they may be recovered without proof of any amount.

(b) Special damages are those which actually flow from a tortious act; they must be proven in order to be recovered."

General damages are designed to compensate an injured victim for losses such as pain and suffering, emotional suffering, hardship, or inconvenience. These damages are hard to quantify for everyone and are highly subjective, so the law instructs the judge or jury to assign these damages on an individual basis. The amount of the damage for pain and suffering is based upon the enlightened conscience of fair and impartial jurors that apply the facts and law to that specific claim.[1]

There is an old saying that "[T]he easiest pain to bear is someone else's." There is a lot of truth to that statement. It is a challenge to get a jury to understand the degree of pain and suffering someone experiences because of a wreck - especially when the injuries are not visible. You can show a jury an x-ray of a broken bone and they immediately get it. You can have a surgeon talk about having to cut into the skull and remove a piece of the bone to relieve some of the pressure from the brain swelling. The jury understands that testimony and can see the photos from the surgery. It is a much more difficult challenge to demonstrate why someone should be awarded money damages when their neck is injured in a car wreck - no broken bones, no bulging or herniated disk. The client just has a sore neck that annoys her when she drives her kids to school, does the laundry, washes the dishes, and cooks the family meals.

Special damages must be proven in a specific amount. These types of damages include compensation for:

*Medical bills, including:

- ambulance
- emergency room physician
- radiology
- medical doctors and specialists
- chiropractors
- physical therapy
- prescriptions

This is easy to prove as all of these health care providers/suppliers will issue an itemized statement for the services they provide to our clients.

*Lost wages

Typically, if someone misses a week of work due to a car wreck, it can be proven with a couple of check stubs showing the time missed from work, a doctor's disability slip, and a wage verification form signed by the employer. It can be very problematic, however, if someone misses time from work but is paid "under the table" and there is no record on the books. It gets even messier when there is no mention of this work on the tax returns.

Another challenge is explaining how a lower back injury to a warehouse worker can cause him to miss six weeks of work. The jury starts to get the picture, however, when you tell them the job requires him to lift boxes weighing between 25 to 50 pounds off of the floor and carry them up a ramp onto a delivery truck. This bending, twisting and lifting would further aggravate the back injury. He also cannot do office work because he has a 6th grade education and no office skills. His employer loves him, admires his work ethic, but does not have a job that can accommodate him with his 10 pound lifting restrictions, so he misses time from work without pay. He should be compensated for these lost earnings.

* Transportation costs

You would not have to be driving around from doctor's appointments to physical therapy to the pharmacy to get your prescription filled if the Defendant had not caused the wreck. This is clearly money that is coming out of your pocket that you would not have lost if the car wreck never happened. You should be compensated for this loss. Gas is expensive. Parking in some of the private lots can also add up. Keep track of your round trip mileage to these appointments and save those parking receipts!

*FUTURE medical expenses

No one has a crystal ball to tell you everything the future is going to hold for you medically. However, doctors can sometimes tell us to a reasonable degree of medical certainty what they anticipate you will incur should you eventually need a surgery or to undergo some additional tests. If these future medical needs would not have been required were it not for the injuries sustained in the wreck, then you should be compensated for these. The key component to making a claim for these future medical expenses is to get a doctor's narrative addressing the medical needs, why they are necessary, how they were caused by the wreck, and the costs of the procedure(s).

Insurance companies do not like to evaluate claims based on "what if's." Some insurers will tell you that they do not factor future medical expenses into their evaluation. If you can produce sufficient evidence to justify the future medical need, then most will at least consider a percentage of the future medical expenses. Mere speculation about the "possibility" that "sometime down the road" you may be a "potential candidate" for some surgery will typically be too speculative.

*FUTURE lost wages

The standard for proving future lost wages is simple, yet can sometimes be a difficult hurdle to overcome. The way a jury measures future lost income is for them to determine what the plaintiff would otherwise have earned in his job or profession **but for** the injury. [2] This can be easy to prove if the injured victim is paralyzed due to injuries sustained in the wreck. For example, he may have been a truck driver with an 8th grade education and no transferrable skills. He can no longer drive a tractor trailer due to the paralysis, and there is no other job that he could get in the work force.

But what if someone loses their job due to injuries sustained in the wreck. Think back to that injured warehouse worker with the 6th grade education. In a previous example, his employer loved him and could afford to hold the job open for him until he could return. Imagine, though, that the employer was not in a position to keep his position open and he had to fire the employee and hire someone who was readily able to work. What happens then? A great argument can be made that the future lost earnings should be an item that the injured victim can claim. The burden of proving this fact is still the Plaintiff's responsibility. The insurance company will argue that the injured worker was fired, not because of the wreck, but for other reasons. We have heard them all:

- fired because of the bad economy
- horrible employee with a bad work record
- too many "no call, no shows"
- prior poor job performance and this was the last straw
- he could have done the job, but he was too lazy to do it or he was exaggerating his injuries and work disabilities to bolster the value of his claim

The future lost earnings cannot be speculative and you must have documentation to substantiate your claims.

Punitive damages: Sometimes the defendant's conduct in causing the wreck or his actions immediately after the wreck are so egregious that the law allows us to seek additional damages known as punitive damages. The purpose of punitive damages is to punish, penalize, or deter the Defendant from repeating the conduct.[3] The plaintiff has the burden of showing through clear and convincing evidence that the Defendant's misconduct was wilful and wanton, malicious, or with such a conscious indifference to the consequences.[4] Please do not think that we can seek punitive damages in all cases. Georgia case law holds that you cannot seek punitive damages for simple traffic violations. (Bradford v. Xerox Corp., 216 Ga. App. 83 (1994)).

For example, punitive damages can be sought in wrecks where:

- The Defendant was driving their vehicle while under the influence of drugs or alcohol. (Cheevers v. Clark, 214 Ga. App. 866, 449 S.E. 2d (1994)).

  There is a legal presumption under Georgia law that you are driving under the influence if the driver's blood alcohol level is above .08.

- The Defendant causes a wreck and attempts to flee the scene of the wreck.

There are too many situations to list where an argument could be made that punitive damages should be awarded. This is an area where you are again highly encouraged to discuss the facts of your particular claim with an attorney that is experienced in personal injury law.

References

[1] Cooper v. Mullins, 30 Ga. 146 (1860).

[2] Southern Cotton Oil Co. V. Skipper, 125 Ga. 368, 54 S.E. 110 (1906).

[3] **O.C.G.A. Section 51-12-5.1 (c).**

[4] **O.C.G.A. Section 51-12-5.1 (b).**

CHAPTER 10 – What Is My Case Worth?

One question I am often asked whenever a potential client calls my firm is "What is my case worth?" This is a great question and I can certainly understand why clients would want to know the answer. They have had their lives turned upside down because of someone else's negligence. They want to know whether or not their bills will be paid, or whether they will be reimbursed for their lost wages, or compensated for their pain and emotional suffering. But the only honest answer that any attorney can give to this answer - especially if the wreck was very recent - is "I do not know." And that is exactly what I tell the clients, but I follow it up with this statement. "There are too many questions that still need to be answered before we can put a value on your claim."

Let me explain this in more detail. In the previous chapter, we talked about the three things we have to prove in order for a client to recover:

1. That someone other than our client was at fault for the wreck;
2. That the Defendant's negligence (or fault) was the proximate cause of my client's injuries and damages; and
3. The extent of my client's injuries and damages, including:

   - past, present and future medical bills
   - past, present and future lost wages
   - the severity of the injuries:

*are the injuries permanent?
*are the injuries disabling?
*will the client be able to continue to work in their same occupation?

   - are we able to pursue punitive damages against the Defendant (or potentially other defendants) because the Defendant's conduct was egregious, or wilful and wanton?

*was the Defendant driving while drunk?
*was the Defendant driving while under the influence of drugs?
*was the Defendant texting while driving?
*did the Defendant attempt to flee the scene of the wreck?

For sections (1) and (2), if the attorney had not done a complete investigation about what happened in the wreck, he will not be able to completely understand who is at fault. The Defendant and the Defendant's insurance company may try and place fault on someone else - or even the potential client. If the defendant was driving while working for an employer, a potential claim could be added against that employer for negligent hiring and retention, or negligent supervision, or under the legal theory of respondeat superior.

If the wreck that injured the client was recent and the client is still treating, there is no way to fully answer section (3). We will not know:

- the dollar amount of the medical treatment as they are still treating.
- whether or not the injuries will be permanent.
- how long the client will be disabled from work.
- or what future medical treatment, including potential physical therapy, surgery, prescriptions, etc., will be needed, if any.

Too many times we receive calls from potential clients. They were involved in a wreck and they thought their injuries were minor and would resolve quickly. The person just assumed they were "sore" and would get better. The insurance adjuster even told them "of course you are just sore. You will be fine in no time." And then the adjuster acts like their long lost aunt that is here to help. The adjuster offers them $500 for their trouble and inconvenience. The injured victim takes the check, signs the release, and then tries to move on with their life. But then things start to unravel. The nagging neck injury becomes more painful. An MRI confirms that the injury is not just a sprain, but the person has a herniated cervical disk that will require surgery. This procedure, the hospitalization, the anesthesia, the physical therapy, the prescription costs, etc., will be tens of thousands of dollars. But here's the problem: the case has been settled for $500.00. Period. Over. No one forced that caller to settle for the $500.00. They person did it on their own free will and accord. They knew the risks when they took the money - or they should have known the risks. Yet they were "hoodwinked" by the adjuster, and now they are faced with the real consequences. It's a difficult conversation that we have more often than not to tell these potential clients there is nothing that can be done when they settled their claim for a meager $500.00. It doesn't matter how much they will incur in bills, lost wages, or the pain and suffering they will experience.

There is another important factor that we must investigate before we can arrive at a value range of the personal injury claim. We have to know what insurance policies are available to help pay for the claim. Let me illustrate this point with this example:

> The defendant runs a red light and crashes into my client's car on the driver's side. Witnesses at the scene confirm that the Defendant was at fault for the wreck and he gets the ticket. My client sustains several injuries, including:
>
> - a fractured left hip;
> - a broken left arm;
> - a broken left leg;
> - several deep gashes to the entire body, including facial lacerations requiring multiple stitches;
> - there is a concern about internal injuries as there is blood in the urine.
>
> My client's husband calls me from the hospital. His wife, a mother of 2 and full time homemaker, is in surgery as the orthopedic surgeon is attempting to repair the hip. He is obviously distraught about his wife and concerned about how well she will recover from the injuries. He is also worried about the exorbitant medical bills that will result from the medical treatments. As his attorney, we share his concerns

about his wife and her injuries and recovery. In addition, we focus on how the bills will be paid by further investigating the claim.

We find that the Defendant was driving a delivery van for his employer. He was in the course and scope of his employment when he ran the red light and caused the wreck and injuries. This means there will be a company insurance policy available for coverage. These policies often carry much higher limits than regular personal policies.

But what if the Defendant was not driving for his employer when he caused the wreck? Under Georgia law, everyone has to carry liability coverage on their vehicle. However, the required limits are only $25,000.00. Our client's medical expenses may greatly exceed that amount just for her hip surgery. What other options are available?

We would also look at our client's personal insurance policies, as well as the policies of any other relative that may be living at their home. Our clients may have purchased uninsured/under-insured motorist's (UM/UIM) coverage on their automobile policies. We review the insurance policy and our clients have the following coverage:

Liability	$1 million	
UM/UIM	$1 million	(uninsured/under-insured motorist's)
MPC	$ 25,000.00	(med-pay)

With this policy, we have the following coverages available to pursue:

- Our client has $25,000 that they can apply to their medical expenses from their med-pay coverage.
- We can pursue the Defendant's liability policy of $25,000.00.
- We have an additional UIM policy available to us with an additional $999,975.00 in coverage.

$1,000,000.00 in UIM

- 25,000.00 Defendant's liability policy

$ 999,975.00

But what if the client did not have UM/UIM coverage? Assume in this fact pattern that my clients lived with her father. He has the following coverages:

UM/UIM $500,000.00.

MPC $ 5,000.00

In this scenario, our client could apply $5,000.00 towards her medical bills under the med pay portion of the policy. In addition, they would have an additional $475,000.00 in UIM coverage:

$500,000.00   UIM

- 25,000.00   Defendant's liability policy

$ 475,000.00

Whenever a potential client calls us for their free initial consultation regarding their wreck, we will ask a lot of questions about insurance - questions about the Defendant driver, as well as questions about our client's own policies and those of any resident relatives. Often, we may not have the answers to these questions for some time. This is yet another factor that must be reviewed when trying to assign a value range to a claim. Sadly, we have seen a lot of situations where the client has extremely high medical bills coupled with significant, disabling injuries. However, the Defendant may only have a minimum liability policy of $25,000.00. If the injured victim has no UIM policies available to them, the most that can be realistically recovered from insurance is limited to only $25,000.00. The defendant is probably not a person with a lot of assets if they only have the minimum coverage, so any chance of getting money out of them personally is remote. Hopefully, this information will allow you to see the importance of carrying UM/UIM coverage on your insurance policy.

TOP 9 FACTORS WE CONSIDER WHEN VALUING A CLAIM:

It is difficult to list all of the items we consider when we put a "value on a claim." Our evaluations are not just based on the facts and the law, but upon jury verdict research, as well as our experience handling over 29,000 claims for injured victims and their families here in Georgia. I can highlight some of the more important factors:

(1)   The impact of the crash

- how much property damage to the vehicles?
- photos of the crash scene?
- did the air bag deploy?
- was the vehicle(s) towed from the scene?
- witnesses to the crash?
- size of the vehicles involved?
- time of the crash?

(2)   The severity of the injuries

- were the injuries visible at the scene?
- was the injured victim treated at the scene?
- was the injured victim transported by ambulance?
- witness statements regarding visible injuries at the scene?
- any broken bones, scarring?
- surgeries or surgical recommendations?
- are the injuries permanent?
- are the injuries disabling?
- photographs of the injuries?

(3)   The amount of the special damages

- how much in medical bills?
- estimate of future medical treatment?
- how much in lost wages?
- estimate of future lost wages?
- can lost wages be credibly documented?
- any permanent impairment from the injuries?
- the type of medical treatment sought for the injuries?
- the credibility of the doctor(s) involved?

(4)   The parties involved

- how likeable is the Plaintiff?
- how likeable is the Defendant?
- age of Plaintiff?
- occupation of parties?
- can a jury identify with either party?
- how credible are the parties?
- can the injured victim be painted as a malingerer, or will a jury believe the need for the treatment and the disability period?
- prior accidents and injuries?
- were any of the parties on the job when the wreck occurred?

(5)   Punitive damages?

- conduct of the parties at the scene of the wreck?
- were drugs and/or alcohol involved?
- any witness statements regarding the parties at the scene of the wreck?
- driving history of the Defendant?
- did the Defendant attempt to flee or actually flee the scene of the wreck?

(6)　Tractor Trailer?

- commercial insurance coverage available
- did the truck driver or trucking company violate any of the Federal Motor Carrier Safety Regulations?
- driver fatigue involved?
- did the driver have a valid CDL (commercial driver's license)?
- do you have the driver's logs / trip reports?
- can you pursue potential claims against the trucking company for negligent hiring, negligent retention, or negligent supervision?
- was the trailer properly loaded?
- was the tractor / trailer in proper working condition?
- was the equipment inspected before the truck driver started operating it?

(7)　The Defendant's insurance company

- what insurance company provides coverage for the Defendant?
- what does the Defendant have in liability coverage?
- has the insurance company accepted responsibility for the wreck?
- has the insurance company paid for the property damage to the Plaintiff's vehicle?

(8)　Plaintiff's insurance company

- what insurance company provides UM/UIM coverage for the Plaintiff, if any?

- what are the UM/UIM limits?
- any MPC (med pay coverage)?

(9)   Where would a lawsuit be filed? (Also known as "venue")

- Is it an urban or rural area?
- what verdicts have been rendered in this county under similar circumstances?
- how often are civil jury trials held in this county?
- will the Plaintiff present well in this venue?
- will the Defendant present well in this venue?
- are either parties well known in this county?

In all personal injury claims, I highly recommend you have your case investigated and evaluated by an experienced personal injury attorney. It is NEVER a good idea to try and settle your claim with an insurance adjuster on your own - especially if you do not have any idea about the full nature and severity of your injuries. They are not in business to try and give you all the cash and benefits you are entitled to receive. You have absolutely nothing to lose by speaking with an attorney for your free consultation on a claim. But just think of all you could lose if you don't!

CHAPTER 11 – Do I Try And Take On Insurance Company AND Their Lawyers By Myself?

So you've been hurt in a car wreck and it was not your fault. The insurance company reluctantly agreed to pay to have your car repaired. You have been going to your doctor for medical treatment and your health insurance company has been paying the bills. Surely this is a claim that you can handle on your against the insurance company and their lawyers, right?

To quote the great college football coach turned commentator, Lee Corso, "Not so fast, my friend!"

There are far too many landmines in this claim than you might realize. Here are just a few concerns:

- Are you getting a fair settlement?
- Will you have to repay your health insurance for any amount that they paid to your health care providers? If so, how much?
- Does the settlement leave open the possibility that their insured could come after you for any damages or injuries sustained in the wreck?
- Do you know if you have to send an "ante litem" notice to the Defendant before you can proceed with your claim?
- Do you even know what an "ante litem" notice is or whether or not it applies to your case?
- What statutes of limitation apply to your claim?
- Do you really have a full understanding of what the future may hold for you medically? And did you get a report from your treating physician(s) to include in your demand package?
- If the claim does not settle, have you irreparably damaged your claim to a point where no lawyer wants to step in and handle it for you?

- Will you know what to do if the insurance company is taking their time getting back with you, or worse yet, completely ignores you?
- Do you have the time to collect, decode, and understand all of your medical records from all of your health care providers?
- Are you available at all times during the work day to make calls and wait for return phone calls from the insurance company or your doctors?
- Will you know how to secure eyewitness statements? What if you can't locate that witness? Do you have the ability, time or resources, to locate him/her?
- Are you comfortable talking with your employer or HR department to get the lost wage information - in a form that the insurance company will understand and not question?
- Do you know what documentation the insurance company needs to FAIRLY evaluate your claim?
- What if the insurance company's adjuster is out of state?
- What if they ask you to sign a medical authorization that allows them access to your entire medical history?
- Do you give them a recorded statement?
- What if you have no health insurance?
- What if the at fault driver had no insurance - or not enough?
- What if you are asked to go to a medical appointment to meet with one of the insurance company doctors?
- What if you had a pre-existing medical condition that was aggravated in the wreck?
- Do you have the time, the temperament, the patience, the knowledge to handle this claim on your own?

I'll give you the same advice I would give anyone calling my office about a potential personal injury claim:

Talk with an EXPERIENCED personal injury attorney about the facts of your claim. If they feel you have a potential claim, then hire that attorney.

If it is a claim that I am willing to handle at my law firm, I tell the client:

> "If you don't hire us, hire someone - but please hire someone that is a specialist in   personal injury claims. You have absolutely nothing to lose by hiring us, but think of all you could lose if you don't!"

CHAPTER 12 – How Do I Choose The Best Lawyer For My Case?

A question I am often asked by people is "How do I choose the best lawyer for my case?"

The hiring of a lawyer is an important decision and can make or break your case in some situations. Here are some tips you can use to help you find the attorney best suited to help you with your claim:

> (1) Find out if the attorney specializes in the area of law in which you need him or her.
>
>> For example: If you are hurt in a car wreck, you don't want to hire an attorney that mainly handles divorce cases or DUI cases. In my opinion, the days of an attorney handling all legal matters from divorces to real estate closings to auto accident claims are long gone. You have heard the old expression - "Jack of all trades. Master of none." I firmly believe this. Laws change constantly. It is very difficult, if not impossible, for an attorney to keep current on the latest happenings in every legal arena.
>
> Attorneys can claim they "specialize" in a certain area of the law, but do your due diligence to verify this. If the attorney claims to specialize in "personal injury" claims, but his/her website lists cases outside the personal injury arena like bankruptcy, or criminal defense, or collection defense matters, then there is a good chance they have not handled or do not handle a lot of cases for car wreck victims.
>
> (2) Find out if the attorney is recognized in your field as an expert <u>by other attorneys</u>.

What awards or honors has the attorney received? For example, I have previously been recognized as a "Super Lawyer" by other lawyers in Georgia. This is an honor given to only the top 5% of attorneys in the state.

Another way to see if the attorney is respected in the field is to find out if he/she lectures to other attorneys around the state in their practice areas. I've taught other attorneys that devote a substantial portion of their practice to personal injury claims how I handle car wreck claims at my law firm.

I, along with Derek Hays at the firm, am a member of the Multi-Million Dollar Advocate's Forum. This is one of the most prestigious groups of personal injury attorneys in the world. Membership is limited only to attorneys who have received a settlement or verdict of at least $2 Million Dollars.

(3) It is also VERY important that the attorney has EXPERIENCE handling your type of claim. Find out how many cases the attorney has handled like yours. You do not want your case to be the attorney's first! For example, at the time that I am writing this book, we have helped over 29,000 injured victims and their families for cases involving serious injuries and deaths in car wrecks, worker's compensation claims, nursing home abuse, and due to defective products or drugs.

(4) I also believe the size of the law firm matters, and not necessarily the number of attorneys the firm has. Let me explain. As attorneys, we are often in court, away from the office taking depositions, or out meeting with experts on our cases. We aren't always available to answer our client's questions. It is important for the attorney to have a knowledgeable support staff to assist you with your questions when the attorney is not available.

(5) Also find out if the law firm uses the latest in technology. At my law firm, you will not see a big law

library because we don't need all of those legal books as all of our legal research is computerized. I have invested hundreds of thousand dollars in state of the art computer hardware and high tech programs specifically designed to better serve our clients needs. When you call, we can instantly access your database to tell you what has happened, and what will be happening with your claim. This process allows us to efficiently handle your case and keep you better informed.

Who NOT To Hire!

Over the years, I have provided expert advice on all of the major network affiliates in Atlanta, including ABC, CBS, FOX, NBC and the CW Network. I also have made guest appearances on CNN's Headline News. As a result of those appearance, I receive countless e-mails from people regarding their potential claims.

I'd like to share with you an email I received from someone that was involved in a car wreck in the city of Atlanta after an appearance on a consumer advocate's show:

****

Jackson from Atlanta asked:

> "In January, I was involved in a car wreck in downtown Atlanta. The other driver was not paying attention and ran the red light. I was taken by ambulance to the hospital and my car had to be towed. The doctors treated and released me and I took a few days off from work to recuperate.

> A couple of days after the wreck, my phone started ringing off the hook. I was receiving calls from attorneys, "legal advisors", and chiropractors - all of them were trying to get me to hire them to represent me in my wreck.

Isn't this wrong? I feel very uncomfortable hiring any of them. What should I do?"

****

What advice did I give to Jackson?

"First of all, this really ticks me off that attorneys - or people acting on their behalf - are out there engaging in this kind of practice. We call these people "runners." They have friends that work in the department that handles police reports. These friends then will sell a copy of these reports to the runners. The runners will next start calling the people who were not at fault in the wreck. Their goal is to refer them to attorneys or to chiropractors to represent them. If the attorney or chiropractor is able to sign up the client, they will pay the runner a referral fee.

This practice is illegal and unethical for attorneys to be out there soliciting cases like this.

An attorney can not approach Jackson and ask him to hire the attorney. This is called "solicitation." Further, we are ethically prohibited from paying anyone else to solicit Jackson to hire our office. Attorneys hire these runners to do their dirty work and deny they had any knowledge this person was out soliciting cases for them.

Some runners will refer the injured person to a chiropractor who will conveniently have an attorney at the office when they arrive for their first visit. The chiropractor will strongly recommend that the injured person sign on with this attorney or they will have to pay for all of their doctor's visits up front. It is a racket and a scam.

What advice do I have? Here are a couple of suggestions:

First - Get the name and phone number of the person that is calling you. Ask them what lawyer they are working with on these cases.

If they deny they are working with a lawyer, ask them what doctor.

As soon as you have the name of the runner, the attorney or the doctor, tell the person calling you that you appreciate the information. You are now going to call the proper authorities and they should not call you again.

Hopefully, they will leave you alone after they hear this.

Second - NEVER, NEVER, NEVER hire any attorney or doctor that will solicit you to be their client or patient. It is unprofessional, unethical and illegal for them to be doing this. Is this the kind of person you want to entrust with your medical care and your legal case?

Everything I do to market my law firm is completely within the rules set forth by the State Bar of Georgia. I let people know that I'm here for them. If they are hurt and have a question about their rights, or the insurance company's responsibilities, I'm just a phone call or an email away."

****

Attorney's Fees & Costs:

I have been practicing law strictly in the personal injury field for 24 years now. The standard fee contract that attorneys use is called a "contingency fee contract." In layman's terms, this means (or SHOULD mean) that there are NO attorney's fees unless there is a recovery on the claim. You should not have to pay the attorney a retainer, nor do you pay him/her by the hour, the phone call, the letter, etc. But like any other contract, you should read the contract and UNDERSTAND all terms of the contract before you sign it!

Keep this in mind as well: the attorney works for you. If you do not feel he is giving your case the attention it needs, then I encourage you to schedule an appointment to meet with him. Make sure both of you are on the same page and time line about what will be happening on your case and when. There are several great lawyers out there handling personal injury claims. Not all of them are great at interacting with their clients and keeping them informed about the work that is being done on their file. Err on the side of trying to work things out with your attorney and get your questions answered.

There may be a time when you do not have a good feeling about the attorney or his office staff that is handling your claim. If your efforts to communicate with him through calls and emails go unanswered, and you feel as though your problems are not resolved, it may be time to move on and get an opinion from another attorney. The fee agreement allows you to cancel the contract at any time - and you don't even have to explain your reason(s) to the attorney. You will, however, possibly be responsible for paying the attorney for the reasonable value of the work performed or he may place a lien on the recovery in your case.

When the case settles, the attorney will also seek to be reimbursed for any costs advanced and expenses he incurred while working on your case. Every attorney charges for these costs and they are necessary to gather the material to present your claim to the insurance company or to prepare your case for trial. These expenses include costs for copies of medical records, traffic citation dispositions, police reports, investigators, or possibly other experts. If a lawsuit is filed on your case, costs could include the filing fee with the court, the sheriff's fee for serving a copy of the complaint on the defendant, as well as court reporter and deposition costs. At our law firm, we advance these costs for our client and pay the providers and experts for their services. We are willing to wait for a successful conclusion of the claim to get reimbursed. This way, our clients do not have to worry about coming our of pocket for

these expenses - especially at a time where they are hurting -
physically and financially.

****

The choice is certainly yours on whether or not you hire an
attorney. Remember - you only have one shot at justice to recover
all the cash and benefits to which you are entitled. I highly
recommend you hire an attorney! Take advantage of the FREE
consultation that some attorneys offer. This will allow you the
opportunity to talk with the attorney to see if you have a good
comfort level - with his knowledge of the law, as well as with his
ability to interact with you in a genuine, caring, compassionate
manner.

CHAPTER 13 – The Demand Process And Settling Your Claim

When you have completed your medical treatment, the doctor will typically discharge you from his care with instructions to follow up as needed. Doctors often refer to this as "Maximum Medical Improvement" (MMI). In laymen's terms, they are telling you that in their opinion as a doctor, you are as well off as you are going to get. Over the years, some of our clients have called us very concerned when this has happened. They will tell us they are still hurting and do not think every thing has been done that could be done to get them better. As I mentioned in the chapter regarding your injuries and medical treatment, this may be the time for you to seek an opinion from another doctor.

If, however, you feel that you have recovered from your injuries, then it is time to start the demand phase of your claim. I have also stressed in this book the importance of keeping up with all of your medical doctors, your medical bills, your lost wages, your prescription receipts, your transportation and parking costs, and any other out of pocket expenses you have incurred due to the car wreck. The reason for stressing this is simple - these materials are needed so they can be organized, reviewed, and sometimes summarized and highlighted for the insurance company in a demand package that will support your claim for money damages.

When our clients call us to tell us they have been released from their doctor's care and they do not feel they need additional treatment, we immediately request a complete copy of all of their medical records and bills from their treating doctors. The doctor's office often times requires that we pre-pay for the records and they will email or fax us an invoice. We quickly pay the invoice and start tracking when the materials will be sent.

Once the medical records are received, we review the entire chart. We make sure the medical records are actually those of our client. Next, we read the medical records to insure they are related to the car wreck. These reports from the treating physicians should list the nature and extent of your injuries, the care you required, reference any prescriptions or referrals given, and should follow the SOAP format we discussed in the previous chapter regarding your medical care. Sometimes, the final medical note (often referred to as the "Discharge Summary"), does not give us a full picture of what the future might hold for our client. At that point, we call the doctor's office to see if he can write a Final Narrative for us. This report should be very clear on listing all of your injuries and the treatment plan provided to you. It should also address whether or not future medical care will be required, the costs for that anticipated future treatment, and whether or not your injuries are permanent. It can be a difficult task to get some doctors to take the time to prepare these narratives when needed, but it is an extremely important document - especially when the injuries are permanent.

In addition to securing the medical records, we prepare a list of the medical expenses our client incurred. These bills could be from any of the following:

- EMT's
- Ambulance
- Emergency Room Physician
- Radiology Bill
- Hospital bill
- ALL charges incurred during hospitalization
- All treating physicians
- Chiropractor
- Physical Therapist
- Rehabilitation Nurses
- Any lab work
- Any specialists, such as an orthopedic surgeon or neurosurgeon
- All prescriptions
- Any support items, such as cervical collars (neck braces)

- Any parking receipts, taxi receipts, or mileage incurred to and from any of your medical appointments.

We also collect the final information regarding your lost wages, if applicable. Our firm uses a form called "Verification of Lost Wages" that we have the employer complete for our client. The insurer may require additional verification of wages, especially if the injured party is an independent contractor. Tax returns can be used to help clarify the lost wages. Things can get a lot more complicated if the injured victim is getting paid under the table and not reporting taxes.

DEMAND PACKAGE

Once we have all of the above-referenced documentation, we prepare a demand package to send to the insurance company. Not all demand packages are alike as there is not a "one size fits all" approach that should be taken on these claims. Every case is different. There are some basic elements, though, that are usually included in all claims:

(1) **Facts about the wreck:**

This is where we describe the wreck for the adjuster. We explain what happened, and let them know how their insured's negligence proximately caused the wreck and our client's damages. We may include citations to Georgia law advising what traffic rules the Defendant violated. If they were driving under the influence, we may include a copy of the video tape where the Defendant was given the field sobriety test by the arresting officer. A copy of the police report is also attached. If we have taken recorded statements from any witnesses, portions of the transcript may be included too.

(2) **Medical Chronology:**

In this section, we include a full chronology of our client's medical treatment. From the very first treatment to the last, we highlight the medical history for our client. We discuss the major diagnoses, the medical tests, and the findings that occurred in the order in which things happened. It is our goal to present this information into a summary that an adjuster can easily understand. Further, if there are any permanent injuries or impairments, or if the doctor anticipates future medical treatment, we include that in this section.

(3)   Itemization of Special Damages:

The next section lists the charges that our client incurred with all of the health care providers and diagnostic imaging facilities. We include any charges for prescriptions, as well as out of pocket co-pays and mileage/transportation costs. Added to the medical damages is a listing of the lost wages for the client due to the wreck.

(4)   General Damages / Pain and Suffering:

The Demand Package also addresses the pain and emotional suffering that our client experienced as a result of the wreck. There are a couple of schools of thought here. One group believes it is good to put in writing all elements of the pain and suffering the client endured (and possibly still endures) because of the wreck. Another group believes that this issue is better discussed in general terms in the demand package, but elaborated more fully when the attorney talks with the adjuster on the phone or at a mediation face to face. There really is no right answer as experienced attorneys can agree to disagree on which is the best approach. In my opinion, I think there is not hard and fast rule on which approach is best, as I feel it is more of a case by case basis. Sometimes adjusters can be hardened to soft tissue injury claims and they will try and group them into one big bunch. This is where the attorney's experience in talking with the adjuster about the specifics really pays off for the client.

(5)   Money Demand

Most of our demand packages include a demand for a specific dollar amount, especially when we are asking the insurance company to tender the policy limits.

There are several laws that will allow pre-judgment interest and penalties to accrue if an insurance company fails to tender a demand for or within the policy limits and a jury renders a verdict for more than those policy limits. There are some settlement packages we send to the insurance company where we do not make a demand for a specific dollar amount. Again, not all attorneys agree on this issue. Some will tell you they ALWAYS put a demand for a specific dollar amount. Others will tell you that too many attorneys ask for way too much money in their initial demand knowing that the amount the case finally settles for is far less. In this situation, they will argue the attorney loses credibility with the insurance company and the adjuster.

Before we send a demand package, we always call our clients and discuss its contents, as well as whether or not we will be asking for a specific sum. We make sure our clients understand that sending the demand should start the settlement negotiation process. Unless there is a time limit for the insurer to respond within the demand, the adjusters normally take up to 30 to 45 days to review the materials - depending on the complexity of the medical records and/or the amount of the demand.

Settlement Negotiations:

When we send a demand to resolve a claim with an insurance company, our experience in handling over 29,000 personal injury cases over the years gives us a range at which we expect the insurance company to settle. There is a common misconception among a lot of people that insurance companies will typically settle your case for 2 ½ to 3 times the amount of your special damages (medical bills and lost wages). This is simply not the case. As we have previously addressed, so many different factors can affect the value of your claim.

The insurance company often comes in with a low-ball settlement offer. Right or wrong, this is just the way it happens. Some adjusters have even shared with us that their supervisors require them to make two or three low offers before they can start negotiating in a "fair" range. This is especially true when the injured victim is unrepresented and is trying to settle the claim on their own. Insurance companies know - based upon their years of experience and all their past settlement data - that if someone has a pile of unpaid medical bills filling their mail box each day, along with other "past due" bills because the injured victim was not able to work, they can often dangle a small financial carrot in front of that person and they will be forced to take it.

This is a big secret that the insurance companies do not want you to know! You will get more money for your injury claims if you hire an attorney! I wrote about this in a best-selling book entitled "Protect & Defend: Proven Strategies From America's Leading Attorneys to Help You Protect & Defend Your Business, Family, and Wealth." A Consumer Panel Survey of Auto Accident Victims by the Insurance Research Council (IRC) in 1999 revealed that:

- Injured victims receive an average of *40 percent more money* just by consulting a lawyer to learn their rights.
- Injured victims receive an average of *three and a half times more money* before legal fees when they hire an attorney to defend their rights.[1]

A free copy of Chapter 13 from the book "Protect & Defend" is included later in this book. Please take the time to read it and you will learn about the 3 Major Secrets insurance companies do not want injured victims to learn.

Honesty matters when dealing with the insurance company. We have spent many years building our reputation and integrity with insurance adjusters and we will never do anything to harm that as our clients are the ones that end up losing. If an adjuster ever catches an attorney (or an injured victim) in a lie about their case, the chances of getting a fair and equitable settlement are slim to none. They will not know what to believe and will deny the claim or try to get a low settlement.

There is no secret formula to a successful negotiation as there are too many factors involved in this process, including:

- what you are negotiating;
- the potential value of the claim being negotiated;
- who is doing the negotiating;
- the personalities of the individuals involved;
- whether or not all parties have all the facts to make a reasonable evaluation of the claim;
- whether the negotiations are taking place by letter, by email, by phone, or face to face;
- where the negotiations are being held;
- time constraints involved in potentially getting the case settled (i.e., does the client need the money to avoid eviction, or is the statute of limitations is rapidly approaching, or is this on the eve of trial.

A general rule you can expect is small dollar settlement negotiations are nowhere near as long, nor complicated, as higher dollar settlements.

It is important to remember these factors though when negotiating a claim:

(1) If you are the Plaintiff, you have the burden of proving what your case is worth. You cannot just say you anticipate incurring $10,000.00 in future medical bills and expect the insurance adjuster to believe you unless you have supporting documentation from your treating physician. This takes proper preparation of the demand package before you start the settlement negotiation phase if you want a reasonable settlement.

(2)   It helps to know going into the settlement negotiations what a good target range is for the value of your case. We often do jury verdict and settlement research to see what similar claims have resolved for in the county where our clients case could be tried. Sometimes, past performance may be indicative of future results. This is not always true, but something that should certainly be considered.

(3)   There is often a difference between what you are willing to settle for and what the insurance company is willing to pay. Believe it or not, reasonable minds can disagree. The important thing to remember again is you have to convince the adjuster as to why your claim is worth a certain dollar amount. You should also be willing to listen (but not always accept) why they adjuster is valuing the claim in a certain range. Prepare to politely argue your point without being "argumentative."

(4)   We think it is important to get to know the adjuster and the defense attorneys on the other side. I can honestly tell you that the substantial majority of people doing this kind of work are genuinely good, honest, and fair people. Sometimes the system in which they work makes it difficult for them to be completely fair and reasonable, but this does not make them bad people. If they are shown respect and dignity throughout the process (as they deserve), it makes it so much easier to get the case resolved for a fair amount. However, all bets are off if they try to take advantage of my client or are a complete horse's ass in negotiations.

(5)   Try not to get too emotional in the process. Trust me - I know this is easier said than done. But you must separate yourself from getting so emotionally involved in the negotiations that you do not listen to your attorney and keep the discussions factual and objective.

(6)   It is a wise client that takes the time to listen. Not only to their attorney's advice, but to the adjuster's arguments. If you take the time to listen to what they are trying to tell you, this may give you a chance to refute their argument with facts or supporting documentation that the adjuster had not considered.

(7)   I've heard it said hundreds of times by experienced judges and mediators - "Settlement is a compromise, not a win or lose situation." It is not to your advantage - nor the insurance company's - to turn the negotiations into a battle and then a war.

(8)   If you cannot get the claim resolved through direct negotiations with the adjuster, then you have some other alternative methods of dispute resolution to you - if the adjuster will agree:

> **mediation**: This is where both sides sit down with an independent, third party that is experienced in personal injury claims. He/she will hear both sides of the claim, and try to bring the parties together and bridge the gap. Everything that is discussed between the parties and the mediator is completely confidential - unless you give the mediator permission to share the information with the adjuster. The mediator cannot be subpoenaed to trial if you can't get the case settled at mediation.

> **arbitration**: in this system, both parties agree to present their cases to an arbitrator (or a panel of arbitrators). These are independent, third parties with experience in personal injury claims. They will hear the evidence in a less formal setting than a courtroom, and will render either a binding or non-binding award in the claim. If the parties have agreed the arbitration award is "binding", then the award that is rendered serves as a final disposition of the claim. Sometimes parties will ask for a "non-binding" award so they can get an

independent valuation of the claim after someone hears all of the evidence.

- If negotiations fail and the parties are not successful in mediating the claim, then you have essentially two options:

1. Settle the claim for the adjuster's top offer; or
2. File suit.

It is important to stress that when a claim is settled, it is final - absent some extraordinary circumstances.

References

---

[1] Hays, Gary Martin, et al. <u>Protect & Defend: Proven Strategies From America's Leading Attorneys to Help You Protect & Defend Your Business, Family, and Wealth</u>. Winter Park, FL: Celebrity Press Publishing, 2012.

CHAPTER 14 – Liens And Subrogation Claims: Who Will Claim They Are Entitled To Some Or ALL Of Your Settlements.

In this chapter, we will discuss medical liens and subrogation claims. These are two land mines that injured victims (especially those that are unrepresented) and their attorneys should be ever so careful in handling. Once the claim is settled, there is still a lot of work to do - especially if the injured party treated at a hospital, or had any of their medical bills paid through Medicare, Medicaid, Tricare, or through a health insurer covered under ERISA. These entities may claim a right of reimbursement out of your settlement if they paid any benefits on your behalf to your health care providers for treatment for injuries you sustained in the wreck. The insurance company will usually condition the settlement of the claim on the premise that the Plaintiff will satisfy all third party liens and agree to indemnify the insurance company for any claims around these liens.

Medical Liens:

Under existing Georgia law, "any medical practice that includes one or more physicians licensed to practice medicine in this state" can place a lien for the reasonable charges for care of the injured person.[1] This essentially means that any facility with a medical doctor in the practice is allowed to place a lien upon your personal injury claim if they provided treatment to you for injuries sustained in the wreck. This lien is not a lien against your property or assets, nor is it a reflection of your refusal to pay a debt.[2] The lien means that the medical provider has a right to be paid out of any settlement or verdict you may receive in your personal injury claim.[3]

In our practice, we see hospitals file liens more than any other type of medical provider. Sometimes, we see the hospital refuse to bill the health insurer if the facility knows there is a personal injury claim pending. They want to be paid the "full amount" of their bill, instead of the much lower "negotiated rate" they have with the health insurance company. We always encourage our clients to send their bills directly to the health insurer as well to try and get the health insurer to pay them. At a minimum, if a lien is filed, we can and always do attack whether or not the medical bills were reasonable and necessary. The last thing the hospital wishes to be accused of, nor engage in, is inflated billing practices.

Bottom line: If there is a valid medical lien filed, the insurance company will not send the settlement check to you unless and until they know the medical lien has been satisfied. We aggressively deal with these liens up front and work with the health care providers to insure we maximize the recovery for our client, while negotiating a fair payment on the lien.

Subrogation Claims:

In addition to the medical liens discussed previously, other companies or agencies that made payments to your health care providers will have their hands out asking for a piece of your settlement pie. Some have valid claims. Others, we typically tell them to pound sand. Below we will discuss those entities we see most often:

(1)   Med-Pay Insurers:

A substantial majority of insurance companies that provide med-pay coverage (MPC) also include language in their policy claiming a right of reimbursement on any recovery you may get in your personal injury claim. In its simplest terms, they claim that if they pay for medical bills caused by someone else in your car wreck and you pursue a personal injury case against that third party, you have to reimburse the MPC insurance company for any amount they paid. This is one of the reasons I strongly detest insurance companies. Think about it. For years, they charge you premiums based upon the risk that you might be in a car wreck and they might have to pay for your medical bills up to the limits of the policy. You get hurt and they pay. But now they want their money back? Do you get your money back if you never get hurt and they never have to pay? NO!

We tell these companies to go pound sand. They have to prove that you were "fully and completely compensated" for your injuries before they have a right to reimbursed. In my expert legal opinion, they will NEVER be able to meet this burden. In reality, they would be incredibly stupid to sue their own insured seeking reimbursement. Of course, every case is different. If a MPC insurer claims a right of reimbursement, please have the matter reviewed by an experienced personal injury lawyer!

(2)   Workers' Compensation Insurers:

If you were injured in a car wreck while in the course and scope of your employment - and your employer was obligated to provide workers' compensation insurance, your medical bills may be paid under this coverage. These workers' compensation insurance companies will then claim they have a right to be reimbursed out of your settlement pursuant to Georgia law.[4] However, the same rules apply. Before the insurance company is entitled to any reimbursement, they have to prove that you were "fully and completely compensated" in your personal injury claim. I spoke on this issue to claimant's lawyers and insurance defense lawyers at the Annual Seminar for Workers' Compensation Attorneys in Georgia back in 2002. In my expert opinion and experience, there is NO way the workers' compensation insurance company will be able to meet this standard so we do not think they are entitled to any reimbursement. Again, every case is different and I encourage you to have the matter reviewed by an experienced personal injury lawyer!

(3)   Medicare:

Medicare is a program that was established in Title XVIII of the Social Security Act, 42 U.S.C.A. sections 1395 et seq., and is funded by the government. Under Medicare Part A, the government is allowed to recover any money paid by Medicare to any hospitals or nursing homes for injuries you sustained in the wreck. Under Medicare Part B, the government is allowed to recover any amount paid to doctors. There is a specific formula that Medicare uses to calculate the amount of the reimbursement. When we see these liens, we always make sure that the medical bills that are included in the lien amount were actually incurred due to treatment for injuries sustained in the wreck. We often see Medicare liens that have unrelated doctors and treatment dates listed as a part of their right of recovery so we work with the processors to correct their records to get the lien amount reduced.

(4)   Medicaid:

Under Georgia Law, the Department of Community Health has a lien on your personal injury claim based upon the amount they paid to your health care providers.[5] With Medicaid, we see the same issues as Medicare liens as they will lump a lot of unrelated charges into those that were reasonable and necessary for treating the injuries sustained in the wreck. I would encourage you to consult with an attorney to make sure you don't pay more than you owe.

(5)   Tricare:

Tricare is a health insurance program that is set up for active duty military, including reservists and retirees under age 65. According to federal law, specifically 42 USCA Section 2651, "[I]f a member of the uniformed services is injured or contracts a disease, under circumstances creating a tort liability upon a third person . . . the United States shall have a right to recover from the third person or an insurer of the third person." We have been successful getting Tricare's adjusters to agree to a reduction when we can prove that a full reimbursement would be unjust, inequitable, and would create a hardship on our client.

(6)   Health Insurance Plans & ERISA:

Most health insurance policies will include the same language claiming a right to reimbursement out of your recovery. The question of whether or not the health insurer actually has a lien that allows a recovery is one that is exceptionally complex. In fact, there are law firms that specialize in representing injured victims and helping their attorneys deal with health insurers that claim they are entitled to reimbursement. These health insurers will argue that they are entitled to recover based upon The Employee Retirement Income Security Act, 29 U.S.C. Section 1001, et seq. (ERISA). The ERISA statute controls employee benefit plans. The big question is whether or not the health insurer paying premiums in your case is governed by state law or federal law. If state law applies, the health insurer would again have to argue that you were "made whole" in your personal injury settlement; i.e., that you were fully and completely compensated, before they are entitled to a reimbursement.[6] If Federal law applies, then you have to negotiate the lien.

The most important thing you should know about ERISA liens is this: if your health insurance company paid any of your medical bills, I highly recommend you speak with an attorney about the specifics of your claim. You could end up settling for what you think is a fair offer only to have the ERISA plan aggressively pursue you to recover the amount they paid.

References

---

[1] **O.C.G.A. Section 44-14-470(a)(4)** and **(b)**, Ga. Laws, 2004, p. 394, effective July 1, 2004.

[2] Id. at (b).

[3] Id.

[4] **O.C.G.A. Section 34-9-11.1**.

[5] **O.C.G.A. Section 49-4-149**.

[6] **O.C.G.A. Section 33-24-56.1**.

CHAPTER 15 – Legal Deadlines

Every state has established a deadline within which an injured victim must settle a personal injury claim, or in the alternative, have filed a lawsuit. If the claim is not settled within that time period, and a lawsuit has not been filed, there is usually nothing that can be done to resurrect the claim and pursue it. This deadline is known as a statute of limitations.

Under Georgia law, the statute of limitations for personal injury claims is set at two (2) years.[1] There are some exceptions which could extend this but the wisest position to take is to err on the side of getting it settled or filed within that 2 year period. If one party in a marital relationship is injured by a third party, the law recognizes that the marital relationship suffers. In this instance, it allows the spouse that was not hurt in the wreck to pursue a claim known as "loss of consortium." The statute of limitations for this type of claim is four (4) years.[2]

There is one other time limit that you should know about if your injuries were caused by the negligence of a city, county or state agency. Under Georgia law, you are required to put the governmental entity on notice of your claim within a set period. This is called an "ante litem" notice. Failure to do so could bar your claim completely so you should not delay in strictly complying with the notice requirements. The deadlines are as follows:

City: Notice must be given within six (6) months of the injury.[3]

County: Notice must be given within twelve (12) months of the injury.[4]

State: Notice must be given within twelve (12) months of the injury.[5]

Please note: The contents of what must be included in these notices vary greatly depending upon which governmental entity is responsible. Your failure to strictly comply with the statute could bar your claim.

If your case was caused by a government agency, do yourself a favor and hire a lawyer experienced in handling these claims!

It is also important to note that not all causes of action have the same two (2) year statutes of limitation. Some actions may have a one year statute of limitations, while others could be much longer. To find out which statute of limitation(s) applies to your case, I highly suggest a consultation with an experienced attorney regarding the specific facts of your claim. You have absolutely nothing to lose by contacting an attorney, but potentially everything to lose if you don't!

References

---

[1] **O.C.G.A. Section 9-3-33**.

[2] **Id.**

[3] **O.C.G.A. Section 36-33-5**.

[4] **O.C.G.A. Section 36-11-1**.

[5] **O.C.G.A. Section 50-21-26**.

CHAPTER 16 – Do You File A Lawsuit On Your Claim?

When all attempts to settle your claim have failed, filing a lawsuit may be your only viable option. And there are a variety of reasons why litigation may be the only option if you want a financial recovery on your claim. For example:

- The insurance company for the Defendant may be denying liability; i.e., they do not think their insured is legally responsible for causing the wreck. In fact, they could be blaming YOU for causing the wreck.
- There could be conflicting witness statements about what happened in the wreck.
- There may be a dispute as to whether or not the driver of the defendant's vehicle was a permissive user.
- If multiple vehicles are involved, there could be finger pointing between the insurance companies as to which driver was at fault or to what percentage.
- Another problem could be with the amount of insurance available. If multiple parties are injured in the wreck, the insurance company may need some help from the court in apportioning the policy limits.
- The proximate cause of the wreck could be something other than the fault of the other driver. They could be blaming a "phantom vehicle" that caused the Defendant to swerve and hit the plaintiff, and then this unidentified driver fled the scene. An insurance company could try and place the blame on a poorly designed road that does not drain properly when it rains and the puddling of water caused the Defendant's vehicle to hydroplane.
- Property damage to your vehicle may be slight. The small scratch on the bumper, when blown up in a photo and placed in front of a jury, can cause people to question how someone could be hurt with little or no damage to the vehicle.

- You may have to file suit because the statute of limitations is approaching. For example, in catastrophic claims, treatment can be ongoing for years. In Georgia, you have two (2) years within which to file a lawsuit or settle your claim. If the injured victim is still treating, and the Defendant has substantial insurance limits to cover potential claims, a lawsuit may need to be filed to allow the person time to assess their medical situation and what the future may hold for them.

- Sometimes clients may have an extensive medical history that pre-existed the wreck. The only way the insurance company can separate past problems from those caused by the collision is to speak with the doctors in a deposition. We will not allow them access to our client's doctors unless we are present for that meeting or deposition.

- Significant delays in seeking initial treatment for your injuries, or big gaps of time in your treatment chronology may cause an insurance company to want to investigate your claim further through litigation. They may want to subpoena records from your employer to see if an on the job injury caused the flare up, or see if a visit to your personal physician reflects an injury at home. The insurance company is looking for anything they can find to diminish the value of your claim against them and their insured.

- The insurance company may not make you any offer, or at least not a fair offer, as they think that delay can work to their advantage. They have the money, but you have increasing medical bills and other financial obligations that cannot be met because you are not working because of your injuries. As offensive as this sounds - and is - it is a practice often employed by insurance companies to coerce injured victims into taking less money.

- If you are an independent contractor and you are making a large lost wage claim that cannot be verified, they may force you into litigation to see if you can provide them with enough proof to substantiate your loss. They will be looking to see if you complied with the law and filed tax returns, as well as checking the legitimacy of those returns.

- If you are handling the claim on your own, they know you are no real threat to them. If you try to file suit on your own, you are even less of a threat because the attorney knows you are not familiar with the rules of evidence or what it takes to get a fair recovery for your injuries. Think about it. Trial lawyers spend three (3) years in law school learning the rules of evidence and trial techniques. They attend continuing education seminars all the time to stay up to date - on the latest evidentiary rulings, as well as tactics other defense lawyers have used to defeat or minimize the claims of others. Do you really feel like you are competent to battle these attorneys on your own?

The focus of what happens whenever a case is litigated is well beyond the focus of this book. There are many outstanding books written about each aspect of the litigation process - from "Writing Your Complaint", to "Discovery Techniques", to "How To Pick A Jury", to "Opening Statements", to "Cross Examination" and even post-trial motions. The purpose of this chapter is to simply give you an over-view of what you can expect if your case goes into litigation.

(1) **Time Frame**:

If, after discussing the pros and cons of litigation with your attorney, you decide that you want to litigate your case, please do not expect the process to move quickly. It will typically take your attorney two to three weeks to draft the Complaint with facts specific to your claim, as well as to craft discovery materials that address the facts in dispute in your case. Once the Complaint - or lawsuit - is filed with the court, the sheriff's deputy has to serve the defendant with a copy of it. This can be easier said than done. Some defendants are difficult, if not impossible, to locate. Others may try and evade service. You might then be forced to hire a special process server to give the papers to the defendant. Once the defendant is served, he has 30 days within which to file his Answer to the lawsuit. The

Answer is simply his response to the allegations that you have made in your complaint.

When the Answer is filed, the discovery phase begins. This is typically 6 months in our state and superior courts, unless altered by agreement of the parties or the court. During this discovery phase, your attorney can send:

- Interrogatories: These are written questions to which the defendant must provide a written answer, under oath.
- Request for Production of Documents: This is a written list of items your attorney needs from the Defendant to further evaluate the claim.
- Request For Admission Of Facts: This is a list of facts that your attorney prepares about the case. The defendant has to either Admit the fact is true, Deny the fact, or answer they do not have enough information to admit or deny.

This written discovery will often times help narrow the issues in dispute.

Another thing that can be sent is called a Third Party Request For Documents. Either party can send these out to individuals, companies, or any other entity that is not a party to the lawsuit. Defense attorneys will often send these to our client's employer(s), as well as to any of the doctors that the client has seen - not only for the injuries sustained in the wreck, but for any reason. Again, they are looking for other accidents or injuries that were not mentioned in the discovery responses or in the treating physicians' medical records.

Depositions may also be taken of the parties or other witnesses. A deposition is a formal question and answer period under oath. The witness is sworn in before a court reporter, and the attorneys ask the witness questions. When the deposition is over, the court reporter transcribes the testimony into a booklet form. Depositions are almost always taken of the plaintiff. Sometimes the Defendant is deposed, as well as treating physicians, employers, or witnesses.

At the end of the discovery period, the case is stipulated to the trial calendar. This can be done at the request of the parties, or by the court. This is yet another cause for delay. The civil court system has a large backlog of cases - especially in the rural areas. Delays are not because of personal injury claims, but because of other cases such as business to business disputes, divorce cases, collection cases, or real estate disputes. Some counties may not have civil jury trial calendars but two or three times a year for only a one or two week period. Your case falls in line behind all of the other cases that have been filed and stipulated to trial before yours. As you might imagine, these delays benefit the insurance companies instead of the injured victim.

(2)   **Costs of Litigation**:

Litigating a case is not cheap. In addition to the filing fee and the service fee charged by the court, deposition costs and expert witness fees can literally cost thousands of dollars. The treating physicians will want to be paid ahead of time to review your chart, sit for the deposition, or attend a trial on your behalf. They will want to be paid for their time and services - even if you do not win your case. If your case does not settle before trial during the discovery phase, you could also have court costs for the court reporter's services.

(3)   **Risks of litigation / trial**:

No one ever, ever knows what will happen when a case goes to a jury. It is difficult to get 6 to 12 people to agree on where they are going to eat lunch together for one day. Imagine how tough it is to get them to agree on whether or not you are entitled to receive money damages, and if so, for how much. It is certainly a risk if there is a reasonable offer on the table to gamble it to try and get more. This is where it is extremely important for you to rely on the advice and experience of your attorney.

(4)   **Post Trial Delays**:

You may win a verdict at trial, but the insurance company will more than likely appeal. They could allege that the judge made rulings from the bench which were incorrect under Georgia law, and those rulings prejudiced their case. They could allege harmful errors occurred before or during the trial that wrongly effect the outcome, such as:

- improper jury strikes allowed by the judge
- incorrect rulings on Motions To Exclude Evidence
- failure to allow evidence or testimony at trial
- incorrect jury charges being given to the jury before or during deliberations.

The sky is the limit on what they can - and do - allege. These post trial motions and appeals may be done for valid reasons. The net result is still bad for you - further delay in you getting paid.

Litigation is not to be entered into lightly. I highly encourage you to sit down with your attorney - or at a minimum have a phone conference with him/her, and candidly discuss the costs vs. the benefits of litigation to see if it is a valid option for you and your claim.

CHAPTER 17 - Conclusion

Three final things I want to stress to everyone that reads this book:

1. This book is just a starting point for you to learn about your car wreck claim. Hopefully, it will provide you with the information you need so you can openly discuss the facts and the law as it applies to your claim with your personal injury attorney. Remember: No two cases are alike and this book is not and cannot be a "one size fits all" manual that applies to every car wreck claim in Georgia. Nothing can replace you taking the time to have the specific facts of your case thoroughly discussed with an experienced personal injury lawyer.

2. For the attorneys that practice personal injury law in Georgia - and do it the right way, I sincerely thank you and applaud you! Thank you for not using runners or for "chasing ambulances." Thank you for taking up the fight to be an advocate for the injured consumer. This battle is truly one between David and Goliath, but it is worth it. This book was written for you just as much as it was for the injured victims. Please read it and use it and give me your feedback. Though no portion of the book can be copied or used in any way without my express permission, you are authorized to use the forms at the end of this book. Should you have any questions, please do not hesitate to contact me.

3. THANK YOU FOR BUYING THIS BOOK!!!

All proceeds from the sale of this book will go to benefit "Let's Protect Our Kids", a program of Keep Georgia Safe.org, a 501(c)(3) charitable organization with the mission to provide safety education and crime prevention training to our families. Your purchase of this book allows us to educate more families on how to be safe, as well as to fund the training of more police officers in Child Abduction Response Team, or CART. We sincerely thank you for your generosity!

To find out more, visit www.KeepGeorgiaSafe.org.

BONUS CHAPTER – Protect And Defend
3 Major Secrets The Insurance Company Doesn't Want You To Know About Your Personal Injury Claim:
A Former Insurance Company Lawyer Reveals All

"Speak up for those who cannot speak up for themselves, for the rights of all who are destitute. Speak up and judge fairly; defend the rights of the poor and needy." ~ Proverbs 31: 8, 9

When a client enters my law firm, they see this quote from the Book of Proverbs in the Old Testament mounted by the front door. It's a mission statement for my law firm. As attorneys, it's a privilege to help our clients "right" their "wrongs," and not something we take lightly.

There's an old legal maxim: "Everyone has a right to an attorney."

At my firm, we live by this variation:

> "Everyone has a right to an attorney. However, they do not have the right to have MY LAW FIRM as their attorneys."

We must believe in our clients before we agree to accept the case. If we don't think they have a valid claim or are pursuing their case for the wrong reasons, we politely decline to represent them.

This wasn't always the case in my professional career. When I first started practicing law, I worked for a law firm that represented insurance companies. It was our job to defend people that caused automobile wrecks. We couldn't decline to represent someone unless there was a conflict of interest. Even if the defendant was driving drunk, plowed into a school bus full of kids, and had no remorse, we couldn't refuse to defend the case.

This experience working for insurance companies wasn't all bad or a waste of time, as I learned many valuable lessons. With more than 23 years of experience, I've learned a lot about personal injury claims. I want to give you a peek behind the curtain and share three major secrets the insurance companies don't want you to know.

Secret #1: You'll Get More Money For Your Injury Claims If You HIre An Attorney

Insurance adjusters are trained to act like your long-lost friend. They'll say, "You don't need an attorney! We're here to help. An attorney won't be able to get you more money." Please don't fall for this trick if you or a family member has been hurt in a wreck!

In 1999, a Consumer Panel Survey of Auto Accident Victims by the Insurance Research Council (IRC) tells a much different story insurers don't want you to know:

• Injured victims receive an average of *40 percent more money* just by consulting a lawyer to learn their rights.

• Injured victims receive an average of *three and a half times more money* before legal fees when they hire an attorney to defend their rights!

(Stats from 1999 IRC report "Paying for Auto Injuries")

The insurance company won't explain your *rights* to you. The insurer is also not going to explain their *responsibilities* to you. You need an attorney to analyze all potential causes of actions, as well as to help you understand who may be responsible for paying for your claims.

Secret #2: Insurance Companies Practice The 3 D's When Handling Claims

What are the three D's?

- Delay
- Deny
- Defend

There are a few ways insurance companies make money. One is by charging premiums to keep the insurance in force. Another is by taking this money and investing it. I don't criticize these actions; insurers have every right to make money. But there's another way that insurers make money that *is* offensive: When an insurer treats the claims unit as a "profit center," this is wrong. Consider this example: You run a red light and cause a wreck, injuring the other driver. He looks to you to take care of his medical bills, lost wages, and pain and suffering. Your insurance company handles the calls and settles the claims against you. The negotiations at the insurance company are by the claims department. This department sets aside money, called "reserves," to settle claims.

How does the insurer turn their claims department into a profit center? By paying out less than what should be paid on the claim. This is done in three different ways:

1. Delay: The insurance company has the upper hand because they have the money. The injured victim needs money for medical bills or for lost wages. The paychecks stop coming, but the bills do not. When injured victims are bent over the financial barrel, the insurer knows they can get most people to accept less by delaying the claim.

2. Deny: If you submit a claim, the adjuster will allege:

- You're faking your injuries.
- You're exaggerating your injuries.
- If you're hurt, it's because you were injured *before* the wreck.
- If you were really hurt, you should have chosen a "real" doctor.
- You overtreated for your injuries.
- If you've lost wages, it wasn't because of your injuries.

The adjuster never admits that your injuries or claims are due to the wreck. You're just a money-grubbing person seeking "life's lottery" from the insurer.

3. Defend: If you don't like the insurer's offer, or if the insurer denies your claim, you have three choices:

- drop your claim
- accept the low offer; or
- file a lawsuit

If you file a lawsuit, be prepared for the insurer to deny your claims and attack you. Unless it's a case of crystal-clear liability, the insurer will blame you for the wreck or apportion some fault to you. They'll use the courts to delay the claim. Further, be prepared to spend time and money with the lawsuit, and having your entire medical and work history scrutinized by the insurer's lawyers.

On February 7, 2007, CNN's Anderson Cooper wrote on his *360* blog "Insurance Companies Fight Paying Billions in Claims." He asks the reader to assume they're driving down the road when a truck runs into the side of your car, denting the passenger door. You're hurt, but you don't know the severity of your injuries. Your doctor diagnoses soft tissue injuries and whiplash, and sends you to therapy. You miss work, and end up with $15,000 in medical expenses and $10,000 in lost wages. You send a demand to the insurer and ask them to cover just your out-of-pocket expenses of $25,000. You expect the insurance company to do the right thing. But what do you do when the insurer only offers you $15,000 and says "take it or leave it"?

Cooper and his producer, Kathleen Johnston, investigated for 18 months how insurance companies were handling these "fender bender" claims. In particular, they researched how Allstate Insurance Company handled the claim of a woman from New Mexico. She had $25,000 in medical bills and lost wages, but Allstate only offered $15,000. Cooper wrote that "Martinez's case represents what 10 of the top 12 auto insurance companies are doing to save money. And if you're in a minor impact crash and get hurt, former insurance industry insiders say insurance companies will most likely try doing the same to you: Delay handling your claim, deny you were hurt, and defend their decision in drawn-out court battles. It's the three D's: delay, deny and defend." He added that this " 'is a strategy adopted by several major auto insurance companies over the past 10 years,' a lot of lawyers, former insurance company insiders, and others tell CNN."

These insurers are betting most people won't hire a lawyer and will accept the quick settlement offer to go away. Unfortunately, a lot of people do just that. What happens if you take that offer to settle without consulting an attorney? Once you sign that check and release, your claim is over. Some of the most difficult conversations I have with potential clients are when I have to explain to them there's nothing I can do because they waived all claims when they accepted the insurer's check. The adjuster convinced them they were just "sore" from the wreck and most people are fine in a couple of days. "There's no need to see a doctor or hire a lawyer as you will be wasting money," the adjuster told them. "I see this all the time. You'll be fine," she says in a reassuring tone. But the strain of the neck was really a herniated disk that needs surgical repair. The medical expenses alone could be over $50,000. The $500 settlement check that person accepted won't even cover the medications the person will need over the next six months. Unfortunately, there's nothing we can do to set aside the settlement. This happens over and over again—innocent people being taken advantage of by the insurance industry.

So how do you protect yourself?

Secret #3: Don't Sign Any Papers Or Talk To The Insurance Company Before Consulting An Attorney

Here's a quick list of reasons why:

- You could be signing a "Release of *all* claims" without realizing it! The adjuster can tell you they need you to sign a medical release to get copies of your bills and records, but it could also have language on the form that settles your claim. This could be considered a settlement of all claims because you're responsible for reading and understanding anything you sign!

- Another trick is to give you a release that will settle your property damage repairs. You want your car back because you're tired of driving the rental vehicle. "Just sign this release, and I'll have the repair facility release your vehicle. I'll throw in an extra $200 for your hassle." You think the adjuster is being very nice, so you sign the form. But beware, even some property damage releases contain language that could jeopardize other claims.
- The adjuster can ask you to tell her about all injuries in a recorded statement. You mention your neck because it hurts. You also mention your left arm. However, you don't say anything about your lower back because you assume it will quickly improve. Days go by and your back really starts to hurt. You experience numbness shooting down your leg. You seek treatment and find out you have a herniated disk. The doctor tells you that you may need surgery. What happens when you tell the insurer about your herniated disk? They'll replay the recorded statement that doesn't mention the lower back so they *deny* that part of your injury claim. You weren't trying to mislead anyone, or present a fraudulent claim. You didn't know the severity of your injury when you gave the recorded interview. Imagine how it would sound in front of a jury when the insurer's lawyer plays the recording made after the wreck. "I am doing ok. Just hurt my neck and arm." This could be a significant blow to your case!
- Never sign a blanket medical authorization that allows the insurer to get any medical records they want from any medical provider you've ever seen. Even if it is your *own* insurance company, you should limit their ability to collect medical records from medical providers you treated with just for the accident.

If you or a family member has been hurt in a wreck, please realize this important fact about the insurance company: The insurance adjuster that represents the person at fault for your wreck is out to save the insurance company money, *not* to give you the compensation you deserve.

How Do I Avoid Being Hurt For A Second Time After My Wreck?

As a former insurance defense lawyer, I highly recommend discussing your case with an attorney *before* you talk to the insurer. You have nothing to lose by calling an attorney, but think of all you can lose if you don't!

BONUS CHAPTER – Consumer's Advocate
The Mourning After:
Helping Families Cope After A Drunk Driving Wreck

In 1997, I walked into our law firm's conference room to meet an 18-year old young woman, Ann, and her 17-year old brother, David. Their eyes were red and swollen a combination of endless tears, shock, worry, and lack of sleep. Both stood up to greet me, but had difficulty even saying their names without their voices cracking. They told me they had heard about my law firm from friends and stopped by in hopes they could meet with me about their mother, Sandra.

The young woman opened up a folder and slid two things across the table to me. One was a photo of their mother that had been taken a couple of years before. In the picture, Sandra appeared to be in her early 40's, big brown eyes, and with a huge smile. Ann was sitting on one side of her, David the other. Both of them had their arms around their mom. There was still tape on the back of the photo from where Ann had removed it from a frame that sat on a table in their living room.

The other thing Ann handed me was a police incident report. I picked it up to review the details of the car wreck. According to the initial investigation, Sandra left her job at the dry cleaners at 6:15 p.m. She turned left out of the parking lot to go home to cook dinner for her, Ann, and David. She had only driven a 1/4 mile on the road when a drunk driver suddenly veered into her lane, striking Sandra's small Toyota head-on.

The police report indicated Sandra was pronounced dead at the scene. The other driver was not injured. The police officer noted that the other driver, a young woman in her early 20's, was "visibly intoxicated." Several empty beer cans were in the backseat of her car. The driver admitted she had spent the day rafting on the Chattahoochee River with friends and had a "couple" of beers.

Sandra was a single mother taking care of Ann and David. She and her husband immigrated to the United States from Korea years before. He had died in a work-related accident when the children were both very small. Sandra worked two jobs to make ends meet. Now, her children were faced with life without their mother.

Ann and David had so many questions that all families face in this situation. Questions like:

- Why did this happen?
- Where do we begin with funeral arrangements?
- Who will pay for the funeral?
- What about the car?
- What do we do now?

This is a time where you are not only a lawyer, but a counselor. Words of comfort seemed so empty as I could see the pain, the hurt and the worry in their eyes.

The sad reality is that I had been at that same conference room table too many times with family members that had lost a loved one because of a drunk driver. Unfortunately, I have been there many times since. These horrific tragedies happen because of a decision made by a driver to get behind the wheel of their car and operate it after having too many drinks.

It does not matter what you call it:

- DUI: Driving Under the Influence
- DWI: Driving While Intoxicated
- Operating Under the Influence
- Drunk Driving

When you drink and drive, you are not only a danger to yourself, but to everyone on the highway.

Here are some important facts all of us should know about alcohol and its effects:

- 12 oz. of beer = 5 oz. of wine = 1.5 oz. of liquor = All of these drinks contain the same amount of alcohol.[1]
- A driver's impairment is not determined by the type of drink, but rather by the amount of alcohol ingested over a specific period of time.[2]

- Only time can make a person sober. Drinking coffee, exercising, or taking a cold shower will not help. The average person metabolizes alcohol at the rate of about one drink per hour![3]

And these drunk driving statistics are very sobering:

- Every day in America, on average, 28 people die as a result of drunk driving crashes.[4]
- Almost every 90 seconds, a drunk driver injures a victim in a car crash.[5]
- An average of one out of every 3 people will be involved in a drunk-driving collision in their lifetime.[6]

With many years of combined experience representing more than 27,000 injured victims and their families in all kinds of cases, we have handled many, many car wrecks where alcohol was involved. We have amassed a vast amount of knowledge after analyzing the facts and the law in each of these claims. As a result, we think it is important to give our readers advice in three areas:

1. **What can you do to protect yourself and family from being involved in a drunk driving collision?**

Wear a seatbelt!

Make sure every passenger is properly restrained either in a seat belt and harness or in a child safety seat. This is THE most important thing you can do to protect yourself and your family. According to the National Highway Traffic Safety Administration, wearing lap/shoulder belts reduce the risk of a traffic fatality to front seat occupants by 45%![7]

Set a good example for your children by always buckling up EVERY time you get in your car. In most states, you can be pulled over and given a ticket if you are not buckled!

Keep Your Eyes On The Road!

Distracted driving is just as dangerous as operating a vehicle under the influence.

Distracted driving is any activity that occupies or diverts a driver's attention away from the road. *All* distractions are dangerous. All distractions can be fatal. They not only endanger the driver, but also the passengers, other drivers and pedestrians. By far the worst distraction is trying to text message while driving. You are 23 times more likely to be involved in an accident if you are texting while behind the wheel.

Also, when your eyes are not on the road, you are not able to react as quickly if confronted with a sudden emergency. For example, sending or receiving a text takes a driver's eyes off of the road for an average of 4.6 seconds. That is the equivalent of driving the length of an entire football field, BLIND, at 55 miles per hour.

Expect The Unexpected!

Keep your eyes on the road and drive defensively. Be on the lookout for drunk drivers. These drivers may do the following:

- Weave in and out of traffic
- Drift over traffic lines
- Quickly speed up or slow down
- Drive their car without their headlights on at night

If you see any of these actions, stay as far away from the driver as possible. Do not try to get the driver to pull over as you may end up causing a wreck. Try to get the license plate of the car, as well as a description of the vehicle. Then safely pull over and dial 911.

2. **What should you do if you have had too much to drink?**

Let's back up a second. The first thing you should do BEFORE you ever have a drink is to plan ahead. Alcohol clouds your ability to make sound decisions. Therefore, if you know that you will be consuming alcohol, get a designated driver. Make sure that person will honor their pledge not to drink. A designated driver can stand between you and a decision that will change your life and the lives of many others forever.

If you are out and have had too much to drink (or the possibility exists that you could be impaired), DO NOT RISK IT! Call a cab or a friend that has not been drinking to come and get you. Most bars will have a phone number for cabs that service their establishment. NEVER ASSUME you are "sober enough" and can operate your vehicle safely.

3. **What can an attorney do for you if you are involved in a wreck with a drunk driver?**

The answer to this question can be summed up in two very different words:

Punishment and **Compensation.** Let's start with punishment. Drunk driving is a crime and will be punished accordingly.

After a car wreck with a drunk driver, an attorney called a "solicitor" or "prosecutor" will be involved on behalf of the state, county, city, or municipality in order to prosecute the drunk driver for their criminal actions. This attorney may contact you to learn more about the wreck and your injuries. This information will be used by the Judge as one of many factors to determine the severity of the punishment. However, the job of the solicitor or prosecutor is **ONLY** related to the criminal aspect of your wreck and **punishment**.

To receive **full compensation** for the injuries and damages you sustained, you need to contact an attorney that specializes in personal injury and wrongful death claims. This "full compensation" could include reimbursement for your economic losses, such as medical bills, prescription charges, lost wages, etc., and for your non-economic damages, like pain and suffering / emotional suffering. A knowledgeable and aggressive personal injury attorney can do just that for you and your family.

Here are some of the basic steps that must be addressed by the attorney in order to maximize the value of your potential claim:

Investigate All Potential Defendants:

Was the drunk driver driving their own vehicle or driving a vehicle owned by another person?

- Did the person that loaned the vehicle know or should they have known that the driver was impaired by alcohol when they let them use it?
- Was the drunk driver known to be habitually reckless and dangerous due to past DUI charges or dangerous driving behaviors?
- Was the drunk driver on the job when the collision occurred?

Investigate Other Negligent Parties:

- Dram Shop Laws: Most states have "Dram Shop" laws on the books. These laws put potential liability upon an establishment like a bar, restaurant, liquor store or pub if they serve alcohol to someone who is underage and/or visibly intoxicated and that person causes a collision after leaving the business. Dram Shop Laws encourage business owners to diligently and aggressively address the problems caused by impaired drivers. The business can either stop serving someone that is clearly intoxicated and/or make sure that the person does not attempt to drive upon leaving.

- Social Hosts: A social host is someone that provides or allows alcohol to be consumed in their home or at a party they are hosting. The host assumes the responsibility similar to that of a business owner if that impaired driver leaves their party and causes a wreck. It is the responsibility of the host to make sure that none of their impaired guest attempt to drive when leaving the party.

Investigate All Potential Insurance Coverage(s):

The experienced attorney will work to locate ALL available insurance policies to provide coverage to you or anyone else injured in the wreck. This could include all policies that insure the at-fault party, as well as policies you or a resident relative may own that could be a source of additional funds to pay for medical expenses or lost wages.

Punitive Damages:

Punitive damages are designed to **PUNISH** a Defendant for very bad conduct, as well as to deter them from repeating the bad conduct. Drunk driving, racing, and leaving the scene of a car wreck are just a few situations where most states will allow you to seek punitive damages against the at-fault driver.

So What Should You Do To Avoid Being Hurt For A Second Time After A Wreck With A Drunk Driver?

Having previously represented insurance companies, and having handled over 27,000 claims against them over the years, we highly recommend to anyone that has been involved in a wreck—to discuss the matter with an attorney BEFORE you talk to the insurance company. You have nothing to lose by calling an attorney that specializes in personal injury. But think of all you can lose if you don't!

Special Thank You to Contributing Author: Derek Hays

About Derek

Derek M. Hays is a partner in the Law Offices of Gary Martin Hays & Associates, P.C. He has been with the firm since 1996 and specializes in personal injury and wrongful death claims. He is a member of the Georgia Trial Lawyers Association (GTLA). He has been selected by the American Trial Lawyers Association as one of the Top 100 Trial Lawyers in Georgia every year since 2006. He was voted as a "Best Lawyer in Duluth, Georgia" by Legal Force Media Publications.

Mr. Hays is a member of The Million Dollar Advocates Forum, which is limited to attorneys that have achieved single verdicts and/or settlements in excess of a million dollars. He is also a member of The Multi-Million Dollar Advocates Forum for single verdicts and/or settlements in excess of $2 million dollars. Fewer than 1% of all U.S. attorneys are members of these prestigious groups.

In his many years of practice, Mr. Hays has had verdicts and/or settlements published online or in print by Westlaw, Lexus/Nexus, CaseMetrix and Verdicts magazine. He has successfully litigated, mediated, and/or settled thousands of cases in many counties throughout the state of Georgia. He has obtained millions of dollars for his clients in cases ranging from car wrecks to dog bites. He has fought winning battles against all of the major automobile insurance companies throughout the Southeast. While the majority of cases have originated in Georgia, he has also handled cases in Alabama, Mississippi, South Carolina, North Carolina, California, Tennessee, Massachusetts, Florida, New York, etc... He is sworn into all State and Superior Courts in Georgia, Georgia Court of Appeals, Supreme Court of Georgia, and the United States District Court for the Northern District of Georgia.

Following graduation from high school in Panama City, Florida, Mr. Hays attended the University of Alabama in Tuscaloosa. He graduated with a Bachelor of Arts Degree in Communications with a specialty in Advertising. His first career choice took him to Walt Disney World in Orlando, Florida where he spent two years in the Animation Department.

Law school had always been an eventual goal for Mr. Hays, so after two years in Florida, he moved to the Atlanta, Georgia area to complete that goal. He attended John Marshall Law School and completed his studies in two years as opposed to the traditional three year track. While attending John Marshall, he made several appearances on the Dean's Lists and President's Lists for his academic achievements. He won the "Book Award" for the highest grade in many of his classes. He was voted the Vice President of the Student Bar Association for two consecutive terms.

Mr. Hays is the father of two children and is very active in his church, the community, various charities, and his children's school. He has served his church in many capacities from serving on committees to serving Communion on Sunday morning. In the community, he has coached his kids in football, basketball, softball, soccer, and baseball. He was voted in as the Director of Baseball for his local county park with several hundred children involved in the programs. He has volunteered and/or raised money for The American Cancer Society, Keep Georgia Safe, Dream House for Medically Fragile Children, Family Promise, Boy Scouts of America, and the United Methodist Children's Home.

To learn more about Derek M. Hays,
visit: http://www.GaryMartinHays.com. To find out more about Keep Georgia Safe, please visit: http://www.KeepGeorgiaSafe.org or call (770) 934-8000.

References:

1 - National Highway Traffic Safety Administration, "Traffic Safety Facts 201; Alcohol Impaired Driving." Washington, D.C.).

2 - Insurance Institute For Highway Safety. "Q&A: Alcohol: General." Arlington, VA: National Highway Insurance Institute for Highway Safety, March 2012.

3 - Michigan State University. "Basic Alcohol Information." East Lansing, MI 2003.

4 - National Highway Traffic Safety Administration, FARS data, 2010.

5 - Binco, Lawrence, et al., "The Economic Impact of Motor Vehicle Crashes 200." Washington D.C.; National Highway Safety Administration, 2002. NHTSA FARS data, 2011.

6 - National Highway Traffic Safety Administration. "The Traffic Stop and You: Improving Communications Between Citizens and Law Enforcement." NHTSA, March 2001, DOT HS 809 212.

7 - National Highway Traffic Safety Administration Traffic Safety Facts 2008 Data Occupant Protection.

BONUS CHAPTER – Trend Setters
I Will Make A Difference

"One person can make a difference, and every person must try."
~ John F. Kennedy

(...from a speech to a group of students at the University of Michigan
on September 22, 1960 as he was campaigning as a candidate for
President of the United States.)

Within a span of 64 days in 2008, three young women from Georgia
or with ties to the state were abducted and murdered. On January 1,
2008, Meredith Emerson was hiking on Blood Mountain in North
Georgia with her dog, Ella, when she was abducted, held captive for
several days, and then murdered. On March 4th, it was Lauren Burk,
from Marietta, Georgia who was a freshman at Auburn University in
Auburn, Alabama. While walking across a dorm parking lot, she was
forced into her car at gunpoint and later shot and killed. Within
hours of Burk's abduction, Eve Carson, from Athens, Georgia, was
at her home in Chapel Hill, North Carolina where she was attending
the University of North Carolina. She was studying when two men
broke into the house and took her at gunpoint. A couple of hours
later, she was murdered.

These were three very special young women whose lives were
violently cut short. Their murders haunted me as my wife and I have
three young daughters. It made me question if I was doing
everything possible to make them safe in this world. As parents, we
would love to put protective headgear and safety bubble wrap on our
children every time they walk out the door. We wish we could be
with them 24/7 to make sure no harm ever comes to them. But we
can't.

Crime occurs every day in all communities. It does not discriminate
based on sex, race, or socioeconomic status. We see it in pretty
graphic detail when we turn on the television. We read about it when
we pick up the newspaper and we hear about it when we turn on the
radio. If our kids walk into the room, we quickly reach for the
remote to change the channel and hope and pray they did not hear or
see the violence. Your child asks you why you changed the channel
and you simply respond that you wanted to see what else was on TV.

We know crime exists. But when it comes to our family – to our children – we never like to consider the possibility that something could happen to them. Is ignoring the problem really going to protect you and your family? Do you still think the world hasn't changed since you were a kid? Remember those days? Our parents would leave the doors unlocked at night and the windows open to allow the fresh air to gently blow through the home. This was a time when no one would have considered installing an alarm in their own home. We didn't know about mace or tasers or carjackings. The bicycle was our method of transportation, as we would ride it most anywhere at any time and never think twice about it.

Times have changed . . .

There is nothing like the innocence of a child. They think the world is a beautiful place. Why would anyone want to hurt anyone else – especially them? As parents, we always have concerns for their safety and wellbeing. But we don't want to alarm them or over-react, nor destroy their innocence or paralyze them with fear.

So we revert back to denying the problem exists. It could never happen to my family or me. Things like this always happen to someone else. "I know how to be safe", and we re-assure ourselves "I never leave my children alone." We are comforted when we remember that they understand the whole "stranger – danger" concept. We reach for the remote, sit back on the couch, and turn the TV to our favorite reality show.

But let me give you a few disturbing facts. According to the Uniform Crime Report detailing Crime in the United States, in 2009 there were an estimated:

- 1,318,398 violent crimes
- 15,241 murders
- 88,097 reported rapes
- 408,217 robberies
- 806,843 aggravated assaults

So we know there is a problem. We realize our children are vulnerable. We know we are at risk. What do we do to protect ourselves and prevent our families from becoming a statistic?

My wife and I considered enrolling our daughters in karate classes and other self-defense courses. But I felt like this was not really addressing the issue. Sure, I would love for our daughters to know HOW TO DEFEND themselves should the need ever arise, but I think it is more important for them to know HOW TO AVOID ever being in a dangerous situation. It is crucial for me to teach my kids – and all children – how to be PROACTIVE vs. REACTIVE. Awareness is the key! Education is the key! All of us need to know how to recognize the warning signs so we can avoid dangerous situations.

One of my favorite quotes, shown at the beginning of this chapter, is from John F. Kennedy:
"One person can make a difference, and every person must try."

To me, that is a call to action for each of us to get our butts off the couch and do something. Imagine what our world would be like if we all sat back waiting for someone else to make a positive change in this world. It would not be a pretty place.

Motivated to make a difference, I started a non-profit – Keep Georgia Safe – to provide safety education and crime prevention training in Georgia (www.KeepGeorgiaSafe.org). Since being formed in July of 2008, our organization has helped train over 80 state and local law enforcement officers in CART (Child Abduction Response Team). If a child is abducted, the first officers on the scene need to have a step-by- step plan of 'what to do' as time is of the essence in safely securing the child. Why? 74% of the children that are murdered are killed within the first three hours of their abduction.

Keep Georgia Safe has also trained over 70 instructors in the radKIDS curriculum (www.radKIDS.org). RadKIDS is the nation's leader in child-safety education. It provides hands-on learning for children ages 5-12 on safety topics from avoiding abduction to Internet safety to bullying prevention. Bullying has been a hot topic and a reason for all parents to be concerned. The radKIDS bullying prevention model curriculum combines self-esteem with realistic physical skills to escape bullying violence. This is a program that not only stops bullying behaviors, but also empowers children to stop violence physically when absolutely necessary – all with the intent to escape and then report, not hide, the encounter. To date, 73 children have used their radKIDS skills to escape an attempted abduction, and thousands more have escaped the bullying, abuse and violence in their lives.

Keep Georgia Safe has been one of the most gratifying initiatives I have ever started and it really has become a labor of love. I started it and I continue to fund it and volunteer because it is the right thing to do. A lot of people questioned my sanity for starting a non-profit in this economic climate and because I was already a very busy individual. In my law firm, I supervise 5 other lawyers and 30 support staff. And I have already achieved great "success" by most definitions of the word in the professional arena. My law firm has secured over $225 million dollars for our clients in settlements and verdicts since 1993. I have been recognized in Atlanta Magazine as one of the state's top Workers' Compensation lawyers. The American Trial Lawyers' Association selected me as one of the Top 100 Trial Lawyers in Georgia and Lawdragon.com selected me as one of the leading Plaintiff's lawyers in America. I have truly been fortunate.

So why should you get involved with a charity? Here are five (5) amazing things that have happened for me and my law firm as a result of Keep Georgia Safe:

1. It shows a commitment to the community.

Georgia is my home. It's where my wife and I live, where our kids go to school, where our family goes to church. Keep Georgia Safe is a tangible demonstration that I want to do everything I can to make our community – our state – a better place. I have not just given it lip service, but I have done something about it.

Approximately 25 years ago, American Express launched a campaign to increase their cardholder's use of the card and to try and sign up new members. As incentive, American Express promised to donate $1.00 for each new card application to help restore one of the nation's most recognized landmarks, the Statute of Liberty. American Express donated over $1.7 million to the cause. The strategy resulted in a card usage increase of 27% and new applications rose 45%. This campaign clearly showed when a company visibly supports a charity by raising awareness and funds, it can boost sales (American Express, 2003). All things being equal, people will do business with a company that gives back to the community versus one that does not.

According to the Cone Millennial Cause Study, 89% of Americans aged 13 – 25 would switch from one brand to another of a comparable product and price if the latter brand was associated with a "good cause".

2. Opened the door to meet so many incredible, inspiring people.

Because of Keep Georgia Safe, I have had the honor of getting to know some amazing people. Vivi Guerchon, the mother of Lauren Burk, inspired me to start the organization because of her sincere desire to make sure no family will ever lose their child to a violent crime. Ed Smart, whose daughter Elizabeth was abducted from her own bedroom in Utah, has become a friend and very vocal supporter of safety issues and initiatives involving children. He has helped Keep Georgia Safe build awareness for our radKIDS program in this state. Steve Daley, the founder of radKIDS, has helped open my eyes as to the tremendous need for safety education in our country. Sadly, we are too focused on "feel good" programs versus ones that get measurable results like radKIDS.

I have also met so many wonderful people in the State of Georgia that are true influencers – and people that get things done – like Ira

Blumenthal, former President of the Captain Planet Foundation; Vernon Keenan, Director of the Georgia Bureau of Investigations; and so many radio and television personalities that have a chance to make a difference every day that they sit behind a microphone or step in front of a camera.

3. Helped me learn and develop new skills.

I never would have imagined sitting with over 80 state and local law enforcement officers being trained on how to respond in the event a child is abducted in our state. I also never thought I would be helping teach a class of 5 – 12 year old kids on safety topics – but I have done it and I love it! I have honed my speaking and presentation skills through the numerous seminars we have given on safety issues throughout the state.

The media attention our cause has captured has been phenomenal. Our Executive Director, Mary Ellen Fulkus, and I have appeared on 9 television stations, including our ABC, CBS, Fox, and NBC affiliates, 108 radio stations, including the Georgia News Network, and have been in 15 magazines and newspapers. We have made it a top priority to spread the word about being safe to as many people as will listen.

One of the most gratifying stories of success to date happened after one of our appearances on a radio morning show in Atlanta, KICKS 101.5. One of the listeners asked us what we should tell our children to do if they are ever lost or separated from the parent. We told them to stress to their kids to find a mommy or grandmother with children. They will protect that child as if he/she were their own until the parents are located. About a month after the show, we received an email from a mother. She told us about her family's trip to Disney World in Orlando, Florida. To her horror, one of her children became separated from her at one of the resorts. She frantically looked around the hotel. As she rounded a corner in one of the dining rooms, she saw her child standing with a mother and her children. The child had remembered her words of advice and had not left with a stranger. She was very grateful and could not thank us enough for sharing the safety message.

4. Increases a sense of achievement and personal satisfaction.

In the legal profession, it can sometimes take months or even years before a case settles or my client has their day in court. It is the ultimate in "delayed gratification." Working with Keep Georgia Safe, the rewards have been immediate. Parents are so appreciative when we educate them on Internet safety or open their eyes to "out and about" safety issues. The children glow with pride when they complete one of the training sessions in radKIDS and are given positive feedback. I know that every person we touch with our message of safety gains something from it. No one can argue with our mission.

5. It looks great on your resume!

If you are out looking for a job, please do not just sit back and wait for things to happen. Go volunteer. Get out there and make an impact in your community and you will become visible. I hired one of the paralegals at our firm because she showed enough initiative to come and volunteer at one of our fundraisers for Keep Georgia Safe. I was impressed with her drive, her commitment, and the fact that she was not wallowing in the "poor pitiful me" world. Find a charity or mission that inspires you – and go volunteer!

****

We should all take to heart and practice the old Chinese proverb:

"If you want happiness for an hour, take a nap. If you want happiness for a day, go fishing. If you want happiness for a lifetime, help somebody."

So now I ask this final important question: I will make a difference. **Will you?**

New Client Information Form

Date _____   Mr.___ Mrs.___ Miss___ Ms.___

Date of Accident: _____

State of Accident: _____

Legal Name of Injured Party:

Last: _____

Middle: _____

First: _____

Name to call you by: _____

Maiden Name: _____

Sex: M___   F___

Home Address:

_____

_____

Home: (   )   -

Work: (   )   -

Cell: (   )   -

E-mail Address: _____

Date of Birth:_____

Social Security #_____

Occupation: _____

Job Title: _____

Employer's Name: _____

Employer's Address: _____

_____

Work Phone: _____

Employed since: _____

Single_____ Married_____ Separated_____

Widowed_____ Divorced_____

Spouse's Full Name: _____

Spouse's Work Phone: _____

Spouse's Date of Birth _____

Spouse's SS No. _____

Spouse's Employer: _____

Spouse's Employer's Address:

_____

_____

Parent/Person who is <u>always</u> able to contact you if an emergency:

_____

Name Relationship:

_____

Address:

_____

_____

Home Phone _____

Work Phone _____

Have you filed for Bankruptcy in the last 5 years? _____

If yes, when? _____

Chapter 7: _____ or Chapter 13:

Where was it filed? _____

How did you hear about GARY MARTIN HAYS & ASSOCIATES?

_____

Reason for consulting an attorney?

_____

Car Wreck Questionnaire

Personal and Confidential

<u>INJURED PARTY</u>:

Name of Injured Party: _____

Are you over 18 years of age: Yes _____ No _____

Are you married: Yes____   No____

ACCIDENT

Date of the accident: _____

Time _____

Where did it happen? _____

Please describe how the accident happened:

_____

Were you the driver or a passenger: _____

Were there any other passengers in your vehicle? If yes, please list them:

1.   _____

2. _____

3. _____

4. _____

What police department investigated the accident?

_____

If you have a copy of the police report, please get it to us as quickly as possible.

Were you given a ticket?   Yes_____   No_____

If so, why? _____

When is the Traffic Court Date _____

DEFENDANT

Who drove the vehicle that caused your injuries:

Name: _____

Address:

_____

_____

Who owned the vehicle: _____

Did the Defendant have any passengers in his/her vehicle:

Yes _____ No _____

Was the Defendant Charged?   Yes_____   No_____

If yes, for what was the Defendant Cited:

_____

Did the Defendant make any comments at the scene? If yes, please list them here:

_____

_____

_____

_____

Did the Defendant admit fault?   Yes_____   No_____

Was the Defendant working when the accident occurred?   Yes_____   No_____

If yes, for what company:

_____

Were any other Vehicles involved in the wreck?

_____

DEFENDANT'S INSURANCE

What company insures the Defendant?

_____

Who is the adjuster: _____

Phone No. _____

Claim No. _____

Policy No. _____

Did you give a recorded statement to the insurance company:
Yes_____ No_____

When: _____

Have you settled your property damage claim? If yes, please answer
the following:

Amount of Settlement: _____

When Settled: _____

PLAINTIFF'S INSURANCE   (Primary)

Do you or a family member that you live with have car insurance? If so, please answer the following:

Name of the Insurance Company: _____

Name of the person(s) insured:_____

Policy #: _____

Have you submitted a claim to them: _____

HEALTH INSURANCE

Do you have health insurance? If so, with what company:

I.D. No._____

Is this through your (or your spouse's) employer? If so, please provide the Group # for the insurer:

Group No. _____

<u>INJURIES</u>

Please describe your injuries:

_____

_____

_____

Were you wearing a seatbelt?   Yes____   No____

Shoulder harness?   Yes____   No____

Was your vehicle equipped with an airbag?   Yes____   No____

Were you transported by Ambulance from the scene of the wreck?   Yes____   No____

Did you go to a Hospital/Emergency Room?

Date: _____

Were you Treated and Released _____ or admitted _____?

Where have you been for medical treatment:

_____

Name of Doctor or facility: _____

Address:

_____

_____

Phone #: (_____) _____-_____

Have you treated with this doctor or facility before? If so,

When: _____

Why:_____

Name of Doctor or facility: _____

Address:

_____

_____

Phone #: (_____) _____-_____

PLAINTIFF'S EMPLOYMENT

Were you on the job when the wreck happened? If yes, please explain what you were doing:

_____

_____

_____

Were you employed on the date of the accident? If so, please answer the following:

Name of Employer: _____

Job Title: _____

Rate of Pay: _____

Normal Hours _____

Normal Days _____

Time Lost: _____

Did you work a second job? If so, please provide the following information:

Employer: _____

Job Title: _____

Rate of Pay: _____

Normal Hours _____

Normal Days _____

Time Lost: _____

PROPERTY DAMAGE TO YOUR VEHICLE

Year and Make of Car: _____

Estimate of Damage - Cost of Repairs $

_____

Where is the car now: _____

Was other property damaged in the wreck? If yes, please describe:

_____

_____

Do you have Photos of your damaged vehicle?   Yes_____   No_____

HISTORY

      1.   Previous Accidents or Injuries: (date, description, attorney)

      2.   Have you ever made a claim for injuries before this?

Yes_____   No_____

      3.   Have you ever sued anybody or been sued by anyone?

Yes_____   No_____

      4.   Have you hired any other attorney regarding this incident?

Yes_____   No_____

      5.   If you answered yes to Nos. 2, 3 or 4 above, then give details

Additional Notes:

_____

To Do List:

_____

_____

_____

_____

_____

_____

_____

HIPPA Authorization

HIPAA AUTHORIZATION FOR RELEASE /

DISCLOSURE OF PROTECTED HEALTH INFORMATION

I hereby request and authorize _____ to release records as described below for the purpose of:

___ Continued treatment ___ Insurance ___ Attorney

___ Personal ___ Other

****
****

Patient's Full Name: _____

Date of Birth: _____

Medical Record # (if known): _____

Social Security #: _____

Phone #: (Home): (_____) _____ - _____

(Work) (_____) _____ - _____

Current address:

_____

_____

I further request and authorize the following facilities to release the medical / financial records . .

1. _____

2. _____

3. _____

4. _____

to my legal representatives by mail:

LAW OFFICES OF GARY MARTIN HAYS & ASSOCIATES, P.C., P.O. Box 956669, Duluth, GA 30095. (770) 934-8000.

Further, said legal representatives may receive these records by fax, or may pick them up in person, and may communicate with you regarding said records.

This Authorization applies to the information checked below for the dates of service on or after:

_____

____   Ambulance Record

____   Face Sheet

____   Pathology Slides

____   Consultation Reports

____   History & Physical Report

____   Pathology Reports

____   Physical Therapy / Occupational Therapy Notes (PT/OT)

____   Discharge Summary Reports

____   Emergency Department Records

____   Office Visit Records

____   Lab Test Results

____   Operative Reports

____   Progress Notes

____   Radiology Reports

____   Radiology Films

____   Financial Record

____   Psychiatric Evaluations

____   Autopsy Reports

____   ENTIRE MEDICAL RECORD

____   Other: _____

I understand that the information used or disclosed pursuant to this Authorization may be subject to re-disclosure by the recipient of the information, and may then no longer be protected by the federal privacy regulations. I understand that unless otherwise limited by state or federal regulations, I may revoke this Authorization at any time by presenting my revocation in writing except to the extent that

_____ has taken action in reliance on this Authorization. I further understand that this Authorization is specific to the information checked above, for the date of services indicated, and for the purposes written above. I understand that this disclosure may include psychiatric, drug/alcohol, and/or HIV testing results, and/or AIDS related information. This facility shall not condition treatment on the receipt of this Authorization, except when such conditioning is permitted in the circumstances identified in the policy entitled "Authorization for Release/Disclosure of Protected Health Information."

This Authorization and/or request to release information from my protected health information (PHI) is fully understood and is made voluntarily on my part and includes faxing of PHI. I understand that a photostatic copy of this authorization is as valid as the original.

I further understand that this Authorization is valid for a period of 1 year from today's date and will expire at that time unless an earlier date is written here: _____.

I understand that there may be a copy charge and, upon request, I may obtain the fee schedule.

Patient (or legal representative):

_____

Today's Date:

_____

Lost Wage Verification

EMPLOYER'S VERIFICATION OF WAGES/SALARY AND ABSENCES

THIS STATEMENT COVERS THE PERIOD

FROM: _____

THROUGH: _____

AND FURTHER CERTIFIES THAT:

EMPLOYEE NAME: _____

EMPLOYEE SSN: _____

EMPLOYEE DOB: _____

DATE OF INJURY: _____

Job Title: _____

Dates of Employment:

From: _____

Through: _____

Average Regular Hours worked per week: _____

Normal days worked:

Sunday   Monday   Tuesday   Wednesday   Thursday   Friday   Saturday

Average Overtime Hours scheduled per week:

Dates Absent:

From _____   Through _____

From _____   Through _____

From _____   Through _____

TOTAL regular hours lost: _____

TOTAL Overtime hours lost: _____

TOTAL hours of leave time used: _____

TOTAL sick-time used: _____

TOTAL personal leave time used: _____

TOTAL Vacation time used: _____

(Please enclose an itemized listing if necessary)

For the above period, please state:

Rate of Pay:

per Hour_____ Week_____ Month_____ (check one)

Overtime Pay:

per Hour_____ Week_____ Month_____ (check one)

Bonus Pay: _____

Authorized Representative's Signature:

_____

Name (Please Print)

_____

Title: _____

Date: _____

Employer's Name and Address:

_____

_____

_____

Employer's Telephone Number:

_____

Car Wreck Conference Office Checklist

Client:_____

File #:_____

Date of ax:_____

Companion Files: _____

_____

_____

Date of Conference: _____

****

Client was advised to bring in the following items to the office conference:

_____   Driver's License or some other form of photo ID

_____   Health Insurance Card

_____   Medicaid?

_____   Medicare?

_____ Tricare?

_____ Which branch? _____

_____ Police Report

_____ ALL Medical Bills, records, and business cards from appointments

_____ ALL insurance cards for vehicles at their home

_____ ALL photos of injuries and damage to vehicles

_____ Any correspondence from anyone regarding the wreck

****

EXPLAIN ATTORNEY CLIENT PRIVILEGE IS WAIVED IF OTHERS THAT ARE NOT CLIENTS AND ARE NOT A PART OF THE LEGAL TERM ARE PRESENT IN THIS MEETING.

People in attendance for conference:

(1) _____

____

(2) _____

____

(3) _____
___

(4) _____
___

(5) _____
___

Plaintiff marital status:

Single:_____

Married:_____

Separated?   _____

If yes, when: _____

Divorced?   _____

If yes, when: _____

Consortium claim? _____

Is spouse on the contract?   _____

Issues?

_____

If minors are P's:

Who has custody? _____

Custodian on contract? _____

Issues?

_____

****

Introduce: Attorney

               Sr. Case Manager

               Assistant Case Managers

               Explain Staff Roles:

Different case managers will be working with client depending on
where they are in the process.

Explain Client Responsibilities

****

Questions for client:

(1) Review Police report:

      Is it accurate? _____

      Everyone listed? _____

      Do we need witness statements? _____

      What statements were made at the scene and by what parties:

_____

_____

_____

_____

(2) Prior Accidents /Injuries:

_____

_____

(3) Any accidents / Injuries AFTER this one:

_____

_____

(4) Bankruptcy? When/What type? _____

          Still active? _____

     If yes, name of attorney: _____

(5) Verify all places of treatment:

_____

_____

(6) Verify All injuries:

_____

_____

_____

(7) Verify Employment and lost wage information:

>Review LOW form and disability statement from the doctor.

>Advise client that tax returns may be required to prove lost wages.

(8) Has property damage been resolved?

Amount of repairs: $_____

Total loss? $_____

What company paid to have the car repaired?

_____

(9) Diminished value (if repaired)

Make of car: _____

Model of car: _____

Year of car: _____

Mileage: _____

Any prior
damage: _____

If so, where and how much $: _____

_____

(10) WARNING re: Facebook, Twitter, Instagram, and other social networking sites.

(11) Verify address and name and phone number of emergency contacts.

Other emergency contacts?

_____

_____

(12) Health Insurance

Explain claims of right of reimbursement

(13) Review ALL automobile policies

Any MPC? _____

Explain medpay:

_____

Any UM / UIM:　　　_____

Explain UM / UIM:

_____

****　If no UM, have client sign NO UM
AFFIDAVIT: _____

Any family members living with the Plaintiff that have auto insurance?

If yes, who: _____

What type of vehicle(s): _____

Insurance?　　　_____

(14)   List all Client Questions?

_____

_____

_____

_____

_____

_____

_____

I, _____, hereby certify that
the information I have provided to the Law Offices of Gary Martin
Hays & Associates, P.C., on this date is true and correct. If any of
the information changes, I promise to immediately notify them as I
understand the information could materially effect my case.

I also authorize the attorneys and staff to discuss all aspects of my
claim with the following people:

* _____

phone (_____) _____ - _____

Relationship: _____

* _____

phone (_____) _____ - _____

Relationship: _____

* _____

phone (_____) _____ - _____

Relationship: _____

_____ I understand that the LAW OFFICES OF GARY
MARTIN HAYS & ASSOCIATES, P.C., ONLY represents me in
the claims in which I have signed an Authority to Represent with the
firm. If there are other potential claims against any other potential
Defendants, I understand that I have not hired the LAW OFFICES
OF GARY MARTIN HAYS & ASSOCIATES, P.C., to represent
me. Further, the LAW OFFICES OF GARY MARTIN HAYS &

ASSOCIATES, P.C., has not agreed to represent me in these potential claims, including, but not limited to: Wage and Hour; Race, Age, Sex Discrimination; Sexual Harassment; Products liability; OSHA; Pension Rights; Employee's Retirement Income Security Act; Civil Service and Merit System; Disability or Group Hospitalization Plan; Medical Malpractice; Libel; Slander; Fair Credit Reporting Act; Rights under any union contract; Social Security Disability or SSI; Unemployment Compensation; Legal Negligence; Bankruptcy; Wrongful Discharge; Right of Privacy; Federal Highway Safety Act; National Labor Relations Act; Fraud; COBRA; SOBRA; Garnishments; Negligence of Vocational Rehabilitation Suppliers; Family Medical Leave Act; or the tax consequences or effects of any settlement, including the effect said settlement might have on my Medicare, Medicaid, Social Security, SSI benefits, or the effect on any other Federal or State benefit. I understand that if I wish to pursue these other claims I should do so immediately as there are statutes of limitation which could bar my potential claims if I do not act in a timely fashion. (We have not determined the actual date the statute of limitations runs as this may vary depending upon the nature of the claim as well as the state where the potential cause of action may arise.)

_____ I have been explained the entire claims process and I have been provided with an opportunity to ask any questions that I might have regarding my case.

_____ I understand that no promises of settlement or recovery regarding my claim has been made to me. I do know that the LAW OFFICES OF GARY MARTIN HAYS & ASSOCIATES, P.C., is committed to maximizing the settlement of my claim(s) for me.

_____ I understand that the LAW OFFICES OF GARY MARTIN HAYS & ASSOCIATES, P.C., DOES NOT represent me on any aspect of my property damage claim, including any potential claims for diminished value.

_____ I promise to keep the LAW OFFICES OF GARY MARTIN HAYS & ASSOCIATES, P.C., updated on any changes of my address, as well as my phone numbers. I understand it is important for them to know how to reach me if there are any important events that are happening on my case.

This the _____ day of _____, _____.

_____

Client

_____

Client

_____

Witness

About The Author

About Gary

Gary Martin Hays is not only a successful lawyer, but is a nationally recognized safety advocate who works tirelessly to educate our families and children on issues ranging from bullying to internet safety to abduction prevention. He currently serves on the Board of Directors of the Elizabeth Smart Foundation. Gary has been seen on countless television stations, including CNN Headline News, the BIO Channel, ABC, CBS, NBC and FOX affiliates. He has appeared on over 110 radio stations, including the Georgia News Network, discussing legal topics and providing safety tips to families. He hosts "Do I Need a Lawyer?" on the CW Atlanta TV Network and has been quoted in USA Today, The Wall Street Journal, and featured on over 250 online sites including Morningstar.com, CBS News's MoneyWatch.com, the Boston Globe, The New York Daily News, and The Miami Herald.

He is also co-author of eleven (11) best-selling books "TRENDSETTERS", "CHAMPIONS", "SOLD", "PROTECT AND DEFEND", "THE SUCCESS SECRET", "THE AUTHORITY ON TOUT", and "THE AUTHORITY ON CHILD SAFETY", and "CONSUMER'S ADVOCATE", "THINK AND GROW RICH", "I WILL MAKE A DIFFERENCE" and "THE AUTHORITY ON PERSONAL INJURY CLAIMS" - all of which were released in the last two years.

Gary graduated from Emory University in 1986 with a B.A. degree in Political Science and a minor in Afro-American and African Studies. In 1989, he received his law degree from the Walter F. George School of Law of Mercer University, Macon, Georgia. His outstanding academic achievements landed him a position on Mercer's Law Review.

His legal accomplishments include being a member of the prestigious Multi Million Dollar Advocate's Forum, a society limited to those attorneys who have received a settlement or verdict of at least $2 Million Dollars. He has been recognized in <u>Atlanta Magazine</u> as one of Georgia's top workers' compensation lawyers. Gary frequently lectures to other attorneys in Georgia on continuing education topics. He has been recognized as one of the Top 100 Trial Lawyers in Georgia since 2007 by the American Trial Lawyers Association, and recognized by *Lawdragon* as one of the leading Plaintiffs' Lawyers in America. His firm specializes in personal injury, wrongful death, workers' compensation, and pharmaceutical claims. Since 1993, his firm has helped over 30,000 victims and their families recover over $245 Million dollars.

In 2008, Gary started the non-profit organization **Keep Georgia Safe** with the mission to provide safety education and crime prevention training in Georgia. Keep Georgia Safe has trained over 80 state and local law enforcement officers in CART (Child Abduction Response Teams) so our first responders will know what to do in the event a child is abducted in Georgia. Gary has completed Child Abduction Response Team training with the National AMBER Alert program through the U.S. Department of Justice and Fox Valley Technical College. He is a certified instructor in the radKIDS curriculum. His law firm has given away 1,000 bicycle helmets and 14 college scholarships.

To learn more about Gary Martin Hays, visit <u>www.GaryMartinHays.com.</u> To find out more about Keep Georgia Safe, please visit <u>www.KeepGeorgiaSafe.org</u> or call (770) 934-8000.